GREAT MOMENTS IN PRO HOCKEY

GREAT MOMENTS
IN PRO HOCKEY

Allen Camelli

HENRY REGNERY COMPANY • CHICAGO

All photographs courtesy of *The Hockey News*.

To Imie

ACKNOWLEDGMENT

I am especially indebted to Mr. Kenneth McKenzie, publisher of the *Hockey News, Hockey Pictorial* and *Hockey World*. Without his help, this book would not have been possible.

CONTENTS

FOREWORD

Hockey is a violent game!

Hockey is the world's fastest team game!

It is a game in which men on razor-sharp skates whirl around a rectangular field of ice and body check (ram into) each other while whizzing along at over 40 feet per second.

It is a game in which a vulcanized rubber puck (hard as a rock) jets through the air, head high, at unbelievable speeds of over 120 miles per hour.

It is a game in which players on opposing teams carry big, curved sticks made of hickory which, in time of extreme anger (or even just a bit of pique), can be (and often have been) used to split open the heads of opposing players.

It is a game in which one man—a goaltender—standing firm, must keep that hard rubber puck—which comes flying at him at speeds up to 180 feet per second—from going into an upright net, six feet wide and four feet high. He must stop it with his legs or his hands or his stick. Sometimes, he has to throw his whole body into a cluster of swirling blades to deflect the puck.

It is a game in which players who bleed readily are sought by teams as secret weapons. The more a player bleeds, the longer the penalty for the opponent who opened the wound.

But despite the brutality—or because of it—hockey is the fastest growing team sport in the world. Though first and foremost a Canadian specialty, the game is now exciting crowds from Leningrad to Los Angeles, from Tokyo to Tacoma. No contest, outside the bull ring, provides such a stirring blend of brutality, blood and beauty.

Hockey is as intricate—at times as graceful—as a ballet. But a ballet patterned by two different choreographers instead of one—each working against the other. Each accentuating power and lightness, violence and grace.

Every now and then, the ballet turns into a formless free-for-all. The players drop their sticks, tear off their gloves and start throwing punches. But, in over 100 years of hockey, no one has yet learned to throw an effective haymaker while standing on a pair of skates—thus the damage in these fights is usually slight.

Refined from the ancient European game of Bandy, a sort of knock-down, drag-out wrestling match on ice, hockey became the national game of Canada. There was a lot of ice in Canada and not much else to do in the long winters. The equipment was simple—a pair of skates, a bent stick and any hard object for a puck.

When indoor skating rinks were built, hockey moved inside. And since the rinks were not built to any specifications, hockey was played on some of the craziest lash-ups imaginable. One rink in Ontario even had a band-stand in the center of the ice, adding a wild guessing game to the play—the defensemen never knew which side of the bandstand a puck carrier would take. When one is moving at top speed, this type of guessing game can be dangerous indeed. None of the hockey rinks in those days had surrounding boards, so when a player was checked or went skating off the playing area, the crowd —if he was from the home team—"helped" him back onto the ice. If he was from the visiting team, they roughed him up a bit and then "helped" him back onto the ice.

By the late 1800s, the game had become somewhat more stable. The rulemakers decreed that there would be seven men to a team and that a game would consist of two 30-minute periods. Players were paid as much as $500 per game. The good money, however, didn't lessen the violence. Just about every game wound up in a fight somewhere along the line. One of the main causes of these fights was that the defensemen used to chew tobacco and spit the juice into the eyes of the oncoming forwards. Penalties were plentiful, and many a referee stayed over-night in the arena to avoid being lynched by an angry mob.

The first Stanley Cup game was played in Montreal's Victoria Rink on March 22, 1894. The participants were the defending Montreal A.A.A. and the challenging Ottawa Capitals. Considering the amount of newspaper space devoted to the Stanley Cup playoffs today, the original reportage left much to be desired. The dispatch from Montreal read:

> The hockey championship was decided tonight and never before in the history of the game was there such a large crowd or so much enthusiasm. There were fully five thousand persons present at the match; and tin horns, strong lungs and a general rabble predominated. The match resulted in favor of Montreal by three goals to one. The referee forgot to see many things. The ice was fairly good. [There followed the lineups of the two teams.]

In November, 1917, the National Hockey League was formed. That first year, the league operated with only three teams—the Montreal Canadiens, the Ottawa Senators and the Toronto Arenas. A playoff system was devised by dividing the season into two halves, with the winners of each half (the Montreal Canadiens and the Toronto Arenas, as it turned out) meeting in the finals.

By 1926, the league had ten teams. Four of them— Pittsburgh, Ottawa, Montreal Maroons and New York Americans—later folded. The six survivors—Toronto, New York, Detroit, Chicago, Boston and Montreal—ruled the hockey world until 1967, when six additional teams— Minnesota, Philadelphia, St. Louis, Pittsburgh, Los Angeles and Oakland—were added. Three of these franchises —Minnesota, Philadelphia and St. Louis—are doing fan-

4

tastically well. Pittsburgh and Los Angeles are a little shaky, but still making money. Oakland, although off to a rocky start, was recently purchased by Trans-National Communications, New York. A spokesman for Trans-National said, "We will do all we can to make Oakland a paying proposition."

The next expansion in hockey will probably be global. Russia boasts of countless super hockey players, and, as in everything else, the Russians are ready to take on all comers.

Clarence Campbell, the president of the NHL, believes the future holds world-wide expansion possibilities. He said recently, "It is not inconceivable that the Stanley Cup will be played for in Russia in the not too distant future. . . . the game will expand; the game will improve because the athletes will continue to improve as they have done throughout the last half century."

The NHL is now 53 years old. Included in this book are some of the bone-crushing, rib-tickling, spine-tingling moments that made each of those 53 years great.

1

The Stanley Cup: Hockey's Ultimate Goal

The Stanley Cup was donated to the game of hockey by Frederick Arthur, Baron Stanley of Preston, in the County of Lancaster, in the peerage of Great Britain, Knight Grand Cross of the Most Honourable Order of the Bath.

The Silver Bowl, now known simply as the Stanley Cup, cost exactly ten guineas in 1893 ($50 at that time).

In 1969, a group of Vancouver businessmen were asked to spend $6,500,000 for the right to compete for that $50 cup.

It all began on March 18, 1892, at a banquet given in honor of the Ottawa Hockey Club. During the course of the proceedings, Lord Kilcoursie, a forward on the Rideau Rebels Hockey Club, tapped his glass, asked for the attention of those present, and read a personal letter from His Excellency Lord Stanley, Governor General of Canada. It stated:

I have, for some time, been thinking it would be a good thing if there were a challenge cup, which could be held

7

from year to year by the leading hockey club in Canada. There does not appear to be any outward or visible sign of the championship at present and considering the interest that hockey matches now elicit and the importance of having the games fairly played under generally recognized rules, I am willing to give a cup that shall be annually held by the winning club.

I am not quite certain that the present regulations governing the arrangement of matches gives entire satisfaction. It would be worth considering whether they could not be arranged so that each team would play once at home and once at the place where their opponents hail from.

The proposal was accepted and Lord Stanley, before leaving for England, drew up a list of conditions for the Cup trustees, Sheriff John Sweetland and Mr. Philip D. Ross, who was a noted athlete in his youth and a noted newspaper publisher in later years. Ross remained a trustee for 56 years, until his death at the age of 91.

The conditions were as follows:

1. The winners should give bond for the return of the cup in good order, when required by the trustees for the purpose of being handed over to any other team that may in turn win.

2. Each winning team should have, at their own charge, engraved on a silver ring fitted on the cup for that purpose, the name of the team and the year won.

3. The cup should remain a challenge cup and should not become the property of any team, even if won more than once.

4. In case any doubt should exist as to the title of any club to claim the position of champions, the cup should be held or awarded by the trustees as they might think right, their decision being absolute.

5. Should either trustee resign or otherwise drop out, the remaining trustee should nominate a substitute.

The Stanley Cup was born in 1893—but only to be orphaned in the first year of its life. No one played for it. Although the Ottawa team was hailed as the 1892–93 champions, they were not awarded the cup because the trustees decided that since it was a challenge cup, it had to be won, not just handed out. They ordered the champion Ottawa Capitals to play Toronto's Osgoode Hall team for the privilege of being the first to have their team name engraved on the cup—and they further ruled that the game be played in Toronto.

The Ottawa club refused.

Thus, in the first year of its being, the Stanley Cup was not awarded to anyone.

Because there wasn't a Stanley Cup contest in 1893, Lord Stanley, the man who had donated the silver trophy that still bears his name and is today one of the most coveted prizes in sports, never saw a Stanley Cup playoff game. That same year he was called back to England.

The following year, on February 23, 1894, the trustees announced:

Arrangements have been completed whereby the Lord Stanley Hockey Cup will now pass into the hands of the

Montreal Amateur Athletic Association. Some trouble arose last year about the acceptance and the M.A.A.A. have had it in their possession ever since. The Montreal team will now officially take it over.

No one ever explained how the Montreal club happened to have it "in their possession," but since it did have it, it was the historic Montreal A.A.A. team, and not the Ottawa Club, that was the first to have its name and those of its players engraved on the silver bowl.

In any case, on March 22, 1894, the first Stanley Cup game was played in Montreal's Victoria arena. The participants were the defending Montreal A.A.A. and the challenging Ottawa Capitals.

The teams lined up as follows:

Montreal		*Ottawa*
Herbert Collins	Goal	A. Morel
Allan Cameron	Point	Harvey Pulford
G. James	Cover-point	Heldon Young
Haviland Routh	Forward	Chauncey Kirby
Claire Mussen	Forward	Joe McDougall
Archie Hodgson	Forward	Sam McDougall
Billy Barlow	Forward	H. Russell

Referee: W. Scott, Toronto
Umpires: Messrs. Anderson and Irwin

Montreal won the game 3–2. Five thousand people watched them do it. It was the biggest crowd, up to that time, ever to witness a sporting event in Canada.

The Stanley Cup was officially launched and won.

The Stanley Cup: Hockey's Ultimate Goal

In 1895, the Montreal Victorias took the cup from the Montreal A.A.A. and kept it through 1899. On February 19, 1899, the challenging Winnipeg Victorias took to the ice to play the Montreal Victorias for the cup, in what was to become just about the craziest, most mixed-up game in a long series of Stanley Cup playoffs.

The total score of two games would decide the champion. In the first match, Winnipeg was leading with only one minute remaining. Out of nowhere Montreal came to score twice and lead the series with a one-goal margin.

The second game, played in Winnipeg, was also a slam-bang affair. Montreal was leading 3–2 with 13 minutes still to play. Paul Gingras, the Winnipeg center, picked up the puck behind his own goal and started a mad dash up the ice. He never did reach the Montreal goal. John McDougall, Montreal defenseman, met him at center ice and cut him down with a wicked slash of his stick across the knees.

Referee Findlay stopped play and ruled McDougall off the ice for two minutes.

The penalty caused instant bedlam. The Winnipeg players and their coach insisted that the foul had been deliberate and that Gingras had been completely incapacitated by it. And since he could no longer play, Mc-Dougall, they claimed, should be booted out of the game for good. But the ref had made his call, and like refs since time began, he wasn't about to change it. However, unlike most teams since time began, Winnipeg refused to accept the call. They told Findlay flat out what he could do with his two-minute penalty and walked off the ice.

During the extended "time-out," Referee Findlay went to the Winnipeg dressing room and asked Gingras to show him his knee. One look convinced him that Gingras was indeed seriously hurt.

After Findlay left, McDougall himself came into the Winnipeg dressing room and apologized for losing his temper and deliberately clobbering Gingras.

When told of McDougall's confession, Referee Findlay went back to the Winnipeg dressing room. "Gentlemen," he said, "I have made a mistake. I am sorry for it, but I cannot change my decision. If you are not satisfied with me, I will retire at once from the ice and have no more to do with this game." With that, he went home.

The Montreal club, which was leading at the time, pleaded with the Winnipeggers to continue with another official, but Winnipeg refused, insisting that only the Stanley Cup trustees could appoint another referee.

The fans of those days must have been of a different breed from the modern hockey buff, for all the while this game-within-a-game was going on, the spectators just sat and waited for play to resume.

Finally, a messenger was dispatched to referee Findlay's home. He was talked into returning to the game. Once there, he ordered the Winnipeg team to return to the ice within 15 minutes or forfeit the game.

They reminded him that when he left the arena, his

12

authority in that game ceased. With that, the Winnipeg players went home.

The referee awarded the Stanley Cup to Montreal.

The trustees, Sweetland and Ross, refused to upset the referee's decision, so the result of the unfinished game went into the record book. The Montreal Victorias once again had their names inscribed on the cup.

On January 4, 1903, the Winnipeg Rowing Club and the Ottawa Silver Seven clashed in the third game of a best of two-out-of-three series. Ottawa had won the first game 9–1. Winnipeg took the second game 6–2.

The first 44 minutes of the match were scoreless, but by that time the challengers were so beaten up and battered that Ottawa won in the final few minutes of the game, putting two pucks past the Winnipeg goalie.

While the game was most exciting, it was probably the bloodiest match in Stanley Cup play. The following day, the *Winnipeg Free Press* published a casualty list:

> Hospital cases of Rowing Club: P. Brown, lame; C. Richards, face swollen, leg hurt; C. Bennet, thumb broken, badly bruised; W. Breen, bruised, broken up; J. Hall, cut on head; D. Kirby, cut on head; W. Bawlf, cut and bruised. Seven out of nine injured; two forced to retire from game; three forced to remain in bed after game; one out of hockey for rest of season.

A writer for the *Toronto Globe* had this to say about the Silver Seven:

13

Ottawa players slash, trip and practice the severest kind of cross checking with a systematic hammering of hands and wrists. They hit a man on the head when the referee isn't looking, and they body check a man into the boards after he has passed the puck. The rubber is not the objective, but the man must be stopped at all costs; if he is put out altogether, so much the better.

In 1905, the Silver Seven were challenged by a Dawson City team which had to travel 30 days to appear in the Stanley Cup series. They came by dog team to Skagway, by boat to Vancouver, and then by train to Ottawa. They came a distance of 4,000 miles—only to lose to the Silver Seven in the first game 9–2, and to be slaughtered in the second game, 23–2.

In the second game, Silver Seven's Frank McGee set a record that stands to this day in Stanley Cup competition. He scored 14 goals—8 of them in 8 minutes and 20 seconds.

As for Dawson City—well, it may well have been one of their team members who first uttered the saying that was to become a slogan during World War II: "Was this trip *really* necessary?"

Needless to say, this was not a home and home series.

The Ottawa Silver Seven defended the Stanley Cup through eight consecutive playoffs and won them all.

They had outscored the best teams in all of Canada, 151 goals to 74, and they had lost only 3 Stanley Cup games in 20 played.

The reign of the Ottawa Silver Seven ended in March,

1906. This great hockey team finally went down to defeat in one of the most exciting series ever played.

The challenging team was the Montreal Wanderers. It was to be a two-game playoff, the team scoring the most goals to be the winner.

In the first game, played in Montreal, the Wanderers beat the pants off the Silver Seven by a score of 9–1.

The second game was to be played at Dey's arena in Ottawa. In the opinion of most hockey fans, however, it was merely a formality. A deficit of eight goals was just too much to overcome.

But the Ottawa Silver Seven didn't think like most hockey fans, and right from the face-off in the second game the Silver Seven went on the attack. The Wanderers, enjoying an eight-goal advantage, played defensive hockey. For twelve minutes, the Montreal strategy worked. The game remained scoreless. Then Montreal's Lester Patrick scored the first goal and gave the Wanderers a nine-goal advantage in the two games.

That goal seemed to wake the Silver Seven up. Center Frank McGee got a goal, and Harry Smith, the All-Star forward, added two more to make the score Ottawa three, Montreal one, at half time.

In the second half, Ottawa scored three goals in the first 85 seconds. They were now down 10–7 on the round. Eight minutes later, Harry Smith scored again to make it 10–8. Ten minutes later, Harry fired another and the margin was cut to 10–9. Again, ten seconds later, Smith put another puck into the net, and the series was all tied up. It was one of the greatest comebacks in hockey history.

With eight minutes remaining, Harry Smith, who had already scored six goals in the game, drove the go-ahead goal between the pipes, and the Ottawa crowd went wild. It was pandemonium. However, their cheering was short-lived because the referee disallowed the score on the ground that Ottawa had been off-side.

Then, with only four minutes remaining, Harry Smith was thumbed to the penalty box. That did it for the Ottawa Silver Seven. With Smith out, Montreal put in two fast goals and ended the Stanley Cup reign of the Silver Seven.

"These two final goals sealed the fate of Ottawa's Silver Seven," says hockey writer Henry Roxborough. "At long last, the most celebrated team of its era, and very likely the most esteemed in all hockey history, passed down the road of Stanley Cup champions with heads high and banners flying."

In 1910, Cyclone Taylor, a forward for the Renfrew Millionaires, became the first and only man in Stanley Cup competition to score a goal while skating backwards. He bet he could do it, and, during a game with Ottawa, he took a pass from center Newsy Lalonde and, whirling completely around, skated backward for 15 yards and slammed the puck into the goal.

It was the greatest trick of that or any other year, but

it did not win Renfrew the Stanley Cup. The Montreal Wanderers took it home again that year.

From the day in 1893 that Lord Stanley said "I will give a cup" to the day the National Hockey League was founded in 1917, there had been many rule changes in the game. Blue lines had been introduced to indicate zones, making off-side penalties in the center zone obsolete. Forward passes had been permitted from one area to another. Kicking the puck no longer necessitated a stop in play. These rules speeded up the game, while the introduction of three 20-minute periods, with ten-minute rest periods in between, instead of two 30-minute periods with only one rest period, prolonged both the game and the playing life of the team members.

Three rule changes that were not accepted were those proposed by Mr. T. Emmett Quinn, then president of the National Hockey Association:

1. That, to increase scoring, the puck should be painted green and reduced to half the size, thus making it more difficult for the goalkeeper to see and stop it.

2. That players should be compelled to carry rolls of bills in their pockets, so that major fines could be paid on the spot.

3. That instead of giving a minor penalty, the referee should stop play, take the offender to the side for a half minute, talk to him and try to reform him.

In 1917, the NHL took sole possession of the Stanley

Cup. Since the NHL would have the best players and the best teams, it seemed fitting that they should also have the Stanley Cup.

As we have seen, in its initial season, the NHL operated with only three teams—the Montreal Canadiens, the Ottawa Senators and Toronto Arenas. The Canadiens met the Arenas in the Stanley Cup playoff, and Toronto became the first team in the NHL to have the team name and the names of all the players engraved on Lord Stanley's silver bowl.

At the end of the 1918–19 season, an influenza epidemic gripped Canada. It hit fans and players alike. When the time came for the Stanley Cup playoffs, Montreal had six players in the hospital and Ottawa was barely able to ice a team. It was decided there would be no Stanley Cup winner that year.

Over the years, the Stanley Cup had come in for some pretty rough treatment at the hands of players and fans alike.

After a Stanley Cup win in 1905, some members of the Ottawa Silver Seven were returning from a victory banquet when one of the players, who was carrying a pretty good load of Canadian whiskey, drop-kicked the cup into the Rideau Canal. It stayed in the water overnight. In the morning, a well-hung-over rugby/hockey player returned to the canal and retrieved the trophy.

In 1906, the Montreal Wanderers won the trophy, but when it came time for the presentation, the cup could not be found. Suddenly an Ottawa player recalled: "Sure, I know where it is. Don't you remember, we gave it to Harry [Smith] to take home. He has it."

Sure enough, Harry had it. But it took two hours of searching before it was finally found in a cluttered attic.

In 1907, the cup took another dunking when a player from the Kenora Thistles, incensed at an official's decision, grabbed the cup and threw it into the Lake of the Woods. This time, it was retrieved immediately.

In 1908, the Montreal Wanderers had a team picture taken after winning the Stanley Cup. After the picture was snapped, the team departed, leaving behind the trophy they had worked hard for a year to win. It remained around the studio for some months. Finally, the photographer's mother (she was not a hockey fan, so how could she know what the cup meant?) filled it with black earth, planted geraniums in it and placed it in the window of the studio. But Montreal was a hockey town, and the cup didn't remain in the window long. A passing fan spotted it for what it was and made sure it was returned to its rightful place.

In 1910, the cup turned up in a bowling alley on St. Catherine Street in Montreal. It was filled to the brim with free chewing gum. No one knows how it got there.

In 1924, when the Montreal Canadiens won the cup, their coach, Leo Dandurand, invited all the players to his house for a champagne party. On their way there, a group of the celebrating cup winners stopped their car on a street corner to change a flat, depositing the Stanley Cup on the sidewalk. The tire changed, the group con-

19

tinued on their way, leaving the trophy behind. Upon reaching Dandurand's house, they found they were minus one cup. They returned to where they had changed the tire, and there, right where they'd left it, was Lord Stanley's gift to hockey.

In 1962, Toronto won the cup, but they almost didn't get it. A Montreal fan, Ken Kilander, was caught stealing it. He had jimmied open the glass case enclosing the cup and was staggering out of the arena with the huge trophy over his shoulder (it then weighed 150 pounds) when two ushers spotted him and called the cops. Kilander was booked for disorderly conduct.

It is unlikely that the Stanley Cup will be subjected to any further indignities. In 1964, the cup was 70 years old. It was redesigned, shined up and given a permanent home in a setting that affords it the dignity, respect and protection its age and prestige command. Now the cup that cost Lord Stanley $50 and may eventually cost a Vancouver syndicate $6,500,000 (if they are ever lucky enough to win it) is appropriately housed in the Hockey Hall of Fame in Toronto, where it has become one of the principal attractions.

SHORT SHOT

One night in the early 1860s, a hockey match was in progress in Montreal's Victoria Skating Rink. The puck in use at that time was a hard rubber ball—very much like a handball. As it was belted up and down the rink, it very often bounced over the low boards that surrounded the playing area. Sometimes it would go over with such force that it would break one of the arena windows. After $350 worth of windows had been broken, the manager of the rink had had it. When the next ball was tossed on the ice, he grabbed it. Then he borrowed a sharp knife from one of the fans, cut the top and bottom sections off the ball and handed back the flat center.

The game continued with the newly shaped puck. It slid rather than bounced—no more windows were smashed. And thus the hockey puck as we know it today was born.

2

Maurice (Rocket) Richard: "You Couldn't Have Stopped Him with a Tank"

Although Red Kelly and Gordie Howe have appeared in more playoff games than Rocket Richard, Richard holds, among other records, the record for most goals scored in playoffs, for most goals scored in one playoff year, for the most consecutive games with goals and for the most game-winning goals.

But perhaps the gutsiest goal ever scored by the "Rocket" came in the seventh game of the 1951–52 Stanley Cup semifinals. The score was tied 1–1 in the second period when Richard was crashed to the ice and taken to the Forum clinic, where six stitches were put in his head.

Even though still foggy from the surgery, Richard returned to the ice late in the third period, took a pass from Butch Bouchard, went flying past four Bruins, warded off Bill Quackenbush with sheer strength and hooked a short, one-handed shot past goalie Sugar Jim Henry.

A four-minute ovation followed the goal. Said Lynn Patrick, general manager of the Bruins, "Maurice wanted that goal so badly we couldn't have stopped him with a tank."

Later, in recalling the events of that evening, Elmer Ferguson, then sports editor of the *Montreal Herald,* told a friend, "You know what that guy did—he scored that last goal while he was semiconscious."

Sportswriter Bill Corum called Richard, "The most exciting player ever to pull on a pair of skates."

But the career of Maurice the Rocket Richard was almost over before it began.

In 1940, playing in the Quebec Hockey League, Richard broke his ankle in the first game and was side-lined for the entire season.

About halfway through the following season, he broke his wrist and again rode the bench for the rest of the year.

In November, 1942, while playing with Montreal, Richard was ridden into the boards by Boston's Johnny Crawford and came out of the smashup with his other ankle broken.

At this point, Tommy Gorman, the Montreal manager, was quoted as saying that Maurice Richard was brittle-boned and was being removed from the Canadiens' reserve list.

This was a chance for any team in the league to pick Richard up for free. None did. To all intents and purposes, Richard was through in the NHL.

But Dick Irvin, then the Montreal coach, and a man

with a terrific eye for hockey talent, decided to give Richard another chance and persuaded Gorman to put the Rocket back on the Habitant list.

It was the smartest move Irvin ever made.

From the time his leg mended until his retirement in 1960, Richard gave Gorman, Irvin and the Montreal team —and fans--the best he had. And the best he had was the best there was.

Having finally shaken the major-injury jinx, Richard became part of the famous "punch" line which included Elmer Lach at center, Hector (Toe) Blake at left wing and Richard at right wing. According to hockey writers of the day, this was the best line that hockey ever assembled. It dominated the league until Toe Blake suffered a broken leg in 1948 and had to retire from the game. One hockey writer of the day compared this threesome to a "trio of mad dogs in their savage quest for goals."

During 1943–44, Richard scored 32 goals over the regular season; in the playoffs he netted 12 goals in 9 games as the team walked off with the Stanley Cup. In the semifinal against the Maple Leafs, Richard put on one of the greatest one-man shows in hockey, scoring all of Montreal's goals in their 5–1 win.

During the 1944–45 season, the Rocket became the first man in hockey history to score 50 goals in a season. The previous high had been 44. Richard, with a career total of 544 goals, is second only to Gordie Howe in all-time scoring honors, though he played in 570 fewer games.

But even with all his scoring ability Richard never won

the Art Ross Trophy, which is awarded to the league's highest scorer. And he never won it because although the Rocket could put the puck into the nets with ease, he was not a playmaker, and since the award was given for goals *plus* assists, Richard never had a chance. Another award the Rocket never received is the Lady Byng Trophy, actually the league's good-conduct award. Good conduct was not one of the Rocket's long suits—in fact, the man was downright rowdy. Some of his brawls have taken on a legendary character.

In a game against the Detroit Red Wings in 1951, Richard was rocketing down the ice with the puck when a defenseman's body check sent Maurice head over heels and flat on his back on the ice. The shot went wide. The Rocket, out of his head with rage, charged referee Hugh McLean. "Didn't you see that?" he roared. "I got knocked down and almost had my head split open. Where's the penalty?"

McLean told the Rocket he hadn't seen a thing.

But that wasn't enough for Richard. He continued to protest and kept on protesting until the referee hit Maurice with a ten-minute misconduct penalty.

This should have ended the argument—but it didn't. Not by a long shot.

The incident had Richard all but talking to himself, and the following day, when he spotted McLean in the lobby of New York's Picadilly Hotel, he flipped his lid. Right then and there, he tore into the official. Had not other players intervened, there's no doubt that the Rocket would have really throttled the referee, because when his teammates finally did get to stop the fight, Richard had McLean by the throat. Clarence Campbell, the league president, called this little episode "conduct prejudicial to the welfare of hockey" and fined Maurice $500. It was, at the time, the largest fine ever levied on a player.

Another of Richard's well-known battles with the "establishment" took place the following year. In one evening, he got tossed into the penalty box for threatening to conk a fan sitting in a rail seat in Toronto and then later found himself in the box for fighting with Fern Flaman. This time Maurice considered himself unjustly punished, and figuring he'd justify the penalty, he reached out and belted Bill Juzda of the Leafs, who was standing near the penalty box, with his Sunday punch. Juzda went down as though he'd been belted by Joe Louis and didn't move for a full minute. Richard was tossed out of the game for that infraction.

Two nights later, he scored his 301st goal.

Probably Maurice's most famous (or infamous) clash on the ice took place on March 13, 1955, when he got into a brawl with Hal Laycoe of the Boston Bruins and Cliff Thompson, an official. Richard was suspended for that incident for the rest of the season (the suspension touched off the spark that exploded into the St. Patrick's Day Riot at the Forum—see Chapter 13).

But Richard was seldom censured by his coach, Dick Irvin, for his aggressive conduct. "I can't blame him for blowing up and socking people," Irvin once said. "After all, he's the most illegally held, pushed, battered and elbowed man in the league. It's not unusual to see two defensemen hold him by the sweater while an opposing wing tries to knock the puck from his stick."

Things became so bad, in fact, that Tommy Gorman, Richard's manager, once made a formal protest to Mervyn Dutton, then NHL president, which read in part: "It's quite evident that players are sent out on the ice to trip, hold, wrestle and block Richard by any means. Richard can take care of himself in a standup fight, but they have formed a 'Wreck Richard' club. . . ." Richard was entitled to protection, Gorman declared, and he asked that referees be instructed to give it to him.

Not long after the protest was filed, the Canadiens were in New York to face the Rangers. The New York team had recently acquired the services of one Bob (Killer) Dill, who also had a reputation as a rough guy—so tough, in fact, he had been banned from the American Hockey League for "unseemly conduct." Killer Dill also had a couple of uncles who were pretty good boxers, Mike and Tom Gibbons, who between them had given Killer plenty of training in the manly art of self-defense.

Well, Killer may have known how to box, but he never got a chance to put up his hands that night. Shortly after the game started, a free-for-all broke out, and Richard went after Dill and quickly flattened him with a straight right.

Maurice (Rocket) Richard

When order was restored, Richard and the unconscious Dill were simultaneously dispatched to the penalty box. When Dill came to and saw Richard sitting next to him, he gave the Rocket a shove. Once again Richard uncorked the haymaker, and once again Dill hit the canvas.

All of this, as far as Mervyn Dutton was concerned, only showed that Richard could take care of himself well— so Gorman's protest was forgotten.

The 1957–58 season was probably the highlight of the Rocket's career. He began the season by scoring his 500th goal (Maurice dedicated this puck to the late Dick Irvin —"The man who taught me everything I know about hockey"—who had died in May, 1957) and ended it by the greatest display of skill and ferocity ever shown in a Stanley Cup playoff. Maurice lifted the Canadiens to victory almost singlehandedly, scoring seven times as Montreal blasted Detroit four games to none. In this series Rocket performed the hat trick for the seventh time in his career in playoff competition, a record that could stand forever. And one of the goals that night came under the heading of unbelievable even by those who saw it. During the second period, the Rocket got loose with the puck and came charging down the ice. He was about to get a shot off when defenseman Warren Godfrey caught up with him and wrestled him to the ice. The puck dribbled off the Rocket's stick and rolled slowly toward goalie Terry Sawchuk, who got set to make a simple save. Suddenly Maurice was up on one knee. Using his stick much like a pool cue, he leaned forward and rammed the moving puck past the astounded Sawchuk.

After the game, a reporter asked Detroit coach Sid Abel if he had any new ideas on how to stop Richard. "Sure, I know how to stop him," said Abel. "With a gun."

In his book *Behind the Cheering,* Frank Selke, who spent a half century in hockey and was manager of the Montreal Canadiens, said of Richard: "Of all the hockey players I have ever known, Richard is undoubtedly the greatest. I feel I was signally honored having him on my team."

And the Hockey Hall of Fame must have felt the same way, for in 1961, the year after his retirement, the board of governors took unprecedented action by naming Richard to membership. The rule was that a player had to have been out of action for at least five years before he could even be nominated. The rule had been broken, but as one selector put it: "We all agreed he would eventually be named—so why wait?"

SHORT SHOT

The latest Los Angeles Kings' favorite is a wild and woolly skater named Eddie Shack, who plays the game the way it should be played: with an I-don't-give-a-damn attitude. When Shack first broke into the NHL, it was rumored that he was illiterate. Once, as he was powering his way up the ice toward his target for that night, the Red Wings' goal, a Detroit coach shouted, "G'wan, stupid, you can't even spell."

Seconds later, Shack shoved the puck past the Detroit goalie and lit the red light. As he was skating back to position, Shack skated to the Detroit bench, leaned over the rail to face the coach and, like a child reciting a lesson, said, "Goal—G-O-A-L—goal."

3

Violence and Death

Hockey is a violent game. In its 53-year history, the NHL has seen more broken bones, more busted teeth, more concussions, more lacerations than any other league in any other sport.

Eddie Shore, Boston's bad boy of the mid-1930's, acquired more than 900 stitches in his face and body; he sustained fractures of his back, hip and collarbone. When he quit, he did not have a tooth left in his head. In addition, his nose had been broken fourteen times and his jaw had been cracked five times.

Gordie Howe, who played through 23 seasons of bone-crushing hockey, has been rated by many as the greatest, but he paid dearly for his royal status. He has had over 300 stitches in his face. He has sustained broken wrists, broken ribs, broken toes and a dislocated shoulder. When he was 20 years old, he suffered a skull fracture that almost cost him his life.

Bobby Hull, who has devastated the record book with his fine play and accurate shooting, is also a member of the 300-stitch club. Hull's face is etched with scars. The orbital bones around his eyes have been smashed. His nose has been broken twice. Ligaments in both knees have been torn. In 1963, in a game against Montreal, he had six teeth banged out of his mouth.

One night, in a game at Madison Square Garden, Ching Johnson, probably one of the greatest defensemen the Rangers ever had, got belted in the mouth with a puck. It hurt like hell, but it didn't stop Ching. He finished out the game that night and played another a few nights later. A week went by and Ching noticed he was having trouble chewing his food. He went to see the team doctor and found out that he had a broken jaw. He had played two games with it and saw no reason why he should miss any action. So he had the jaw wired together and was on the ice that night.

For many years, Elmer Lach, Montreal Canadiens' center, was rated as the most injured man in hockey. And considering the injuries to the aforementioned players, Lach must have been really wrecked to deserve that title. One night in a game in Detroit, Lach was involved in a brutal smashup and went out like a light. He was taken to the dressing room, where he regained consciousness. Seated on the table waiting for the doctor, Lach was a horrifying sight. His hair was matted with blood. He looked like death warmed over. His face was pale and drawn. His mouth was parted in a grotesque smile and blood ran down the side of his face.

He was badly hurt. But being the tough guy he was, he scarcely even felt his injuries. "I can't breathe too good because of the blood," he told the coach who was waiting for the doc to finish with him, "but I don't think there's anything really wrong. Maybe if I plugged up my mouth with cotton to stop the bleeding, I could get back in the game."

Ace Bailey of the Montreal Canadiens had his skull fractured in a game but remained conscious long enough to tell his coach that he was sure the man who caused the fracture didn't mean it. (This incident is dealt with in Chapter 15.)

During the 1963 Stanley Cup playoffs, Toronto defenseman Bobby Baun was taken from the ice on a stretcher. No one thought he'd be back in the game. But when the match went into overtime, it was Baun who scored the sudden-death goal that kept Toronto in the series.

The following night, with Carl Brewer, Baun and Red Kelly all requiring needles to deaden pain, the Leafs handed Detroit a decisive 4–0 beating to win their third consecutive Stanley Cup.

Only after the series would Baun consent to have his ankle X-rayed—the pictures showed that he had been playing with a broken ankle.

But throughout all the violence, throughout all the blood and guts, death remained a stranger to the game of hockey.

However, in 1968, and after 51 years of NHL history,

death made its debut, with the fatal injury to Bill Masterson of the Minnesota North Stars.

The untimely death of the 29-year-old center was a crushing blow to those who said, "It can't happen here," and it provided hockey experts with another argument in their long-standing contention that all hockey players should wear protective helmets. Many hockey men are of the considered opinion that the 6-foot, 190-pound Minnesota player would be alive today had he been wearing the fiber helmet that professional hockey stars scorn so readily as "unmanly."

The NHL was shocked to its very foundation by the passing of Masterson in the early hours of the morning of January 15, 1968—from a massive internal brain injury suffered when he was checked and fell heavily to the ice, striking his head as he hit.

Masterson was removed to the hospital, but the injury was too massive for the doctors to operate. As one hospital spokesman put it: "There was nothing we could do to save the boy." Masterson was kept alive for 30 hours by the use of a respirator.

Minnesota coach Wren Blair was stunned by the injury to Masterson, as were the North Star players who saw the incident from their bench.

"It was only a momentary check," said Blair. He also went on to say that there was nothing dirty about the play.

Ironically, it was Blair who had coaxed Masterson back

to professional hockey that season, with the introduction of the expansion teams.

The North Stars' center had quit pro hockey in 1964 to take up a lucrative business position following his graduation from Denver University, where he had received his master's degree. The NHL announced that $60,000 would be turned over to Masterson's estate from the league's pension fund. The North Star player was insured for $50,000 by the NHL.

The death of Masterson was the first mortal ice casualty the NHL had suffered since its inception, although there have been many near-fatal accidents.

And yet, despite the many accidents, despite the death of Masterson, the men in the NHL still go bareheaded.

In fact, while researching this book, this writer talked to many players, retired players, executives and fans of the NHL, and to a man they were against the use of helmets.

"It takes away the color," said one.

"Helmets are for girls," said another.

"You can't recognize the players if they wear helmets," said still another.

Maybe Gordie Howe summed it up best when he was a spectator at a game that was particularly bloody and a fan turned to him and said, "It's pretty rough down there."

Howe shrugged and answered, "Well, it's a man's game."

SHORT SHOT

. . . being the story of the seventh man on the ice.

In the closing minutes of a hockey game, the team that is behind usually removes the goalie to make room for a sixth skater, hoping that with six up-front men going for them, instead of five, they may be able to score the equalizing goal.

And that was exactly the situation, late in the 1968–69 season, when Boston was losing by one goal to Chicago.

With the Boston net open and the Bruins doing their best to tie the game, Bobby Hull came up with the puck and streaked toward center ice. Hockey's number one goal scorer had a clear field ahead of him, and he was on his way.

Suddenly a hockey stick snaked out from the Boston bench and landed between Bobby's legs, tripping him up. Hull shot as he fell, and the puck slid slowly down the ice and into the empty net—the unguarded net.

After the goal was scored, Gerry Cheevers, the Boston goaltender, skated onto the ice to retrieve his stick from between Bobby's legs.

"I know that by doing what I did the referee would have ruled it a goal anyway," he said later, "but I didn't want that puck going into my net."

4

The Golden Hawk and the Golden Goal

It was March 12, 1966. Chicago Stadium was packed to the rafters, and every fan there let out a roar as Bobby Hull skated onto the ice.

He tapped the protective glass at rinkside in greeting to his pretty wife and, with a wave of his stick, acknowledged the ovation from the expectant and adulatory Black Hawk fans, who wanted to see the Golden Hawk go, Go, GO!

The sight of Bobby Hull taking the puck up-ice is one of the greatest spectacles in the sporting world today. It compares with such memorable sights as Dizzy Dean throwing his fast ball; Jimmy Brown breaking the tackle of a linebacker; Oscar Robertson rising straight off the floor for a jump shot; Babe Ruth running the bases after lofting one into the stands; Joe Louis dispatching an opponent to oblivion with his left hook.

But tonight a Hull goal was to mean even more than a red light flashing and a possible Black Hawk victory. It was to mean the shattering of a record that had stood for 21 years and had eluded Bobby through the last three games in which the Black Hawks had been held scoreless.

Just that day, the *Chicago Sun-Times* had run a banner headline which asked desperately: "WILL THE HAWKS EVER SCORE AGAIN?"

Despite such pessimism, there were lots of people who were certain that in the ten games still to be played Bobby Hull would somehow break the hex. Among them were the two men who shared the 50-goal record with him—Maurice Richard, now a Montreal business executive, and Bernie (Boom Boom) Geoffrion, now coach of the New York Rangers.

"When I first set the record," said Richard when interviewed in Montreal, "I didn't think it was going to last very long. But it has lasted 21 years and, if someone has to break it, Hull is the right guy."

"It is hard to compare scoring titles," said Boom Boom Geoffrion, "the quality of play in the league isn't always the same. Hull is a better skater than I ever was and he has a great shot, but I was quicker on the take-off. And I was shooting for the net more often. When Hull first came into the league, you could tell he could be great but he didn't shoot enough. Now he is hitting that net all the time.

"All the players have their eyes on you when you even get close to a record," Geoffrion went on. "You get extra help from your own team but the opposition is playing you harder because they know you're going for the record."

The Golden Hawk and the Golden Goal

And the opposing defensemen had made Hull's path to the record just that—tough. Throughout the league, defensemen and checking forwards made him their target. Ed Westfall of the Bruins stuck to him like glue. In Montreal, one would have thought that Claude Provost was his shadow. Reg Fleming, a former teammate who had helped him score 50 goals in 1962, was assigned as his nemesis by the New York Rangers.

It was Fleming who was all over Hull that March 12 evening. And Reg was doing some job, much to the dismay of the Chicago fans. It looked like another shutout as Bobby Hull and the Black Hawks were held scoreless for two periods.

But then, nearly six minutes into the final period, with the Rangers ahead 2–1, Hull got the curved blade of his stick on the puck on a power play that started well back of his own blue line. He started toward the Rangers' goal. Then, 24 feet from the net, he squared off like Arnold Palmer getting set for a tee shot and blasted the puck right past Ranger goalie Cesare Maniago.

The red light went on, and 22,000 screaming, wild Chicago fans jumped up and went on a seven-minute binge of ecstasy. They littered the ice with debris that ranged from hats (both men's and women's) to confetti.

And as he skated back to the Black Hawk bench, Hull picked up one of the more ludicrous hats and put it on. It got a laugh. The fans screamed even louder.

And well they should have, for there on the ice was Bobby Hull. The Golden Hawk. Mr. Hockey. He had done what no man before in the history of the NHL had been able to do.

He had broken a record that had stood for 21 years. He had scored more than 50 goals in one season.

When asked what they thought of Hull's slap shot, three of the goalies against whom he had scored his 51 —Ken Hodge, Roger Crozier, Cesare Maniago—had this to say in an interview with Stan Fischler in *Sport Magazine:*

Hodge: If he ever hits anybody head-on with his shot, there's a very good chance of him killing him, because that puck is moving something terrible. Let's face it, that wasn't Bobby Hull who hit our Gary Smith in the forehead and Gary still came out of it with a chipped bone. You can imagine what would happen with Bobby's shot.

Crozier: Naturally, I'm concerned with him. And I've been experimenting wearing the face mask in practices, but I keep getting headaches when I wear them, so I don't wear them against Hull or anybody in a regular game.

Maniago: Someday he will kill somebody—whether it's a goaltender or a defenseman or a fan. Someone's going to get it, because now a lot of his shots are not only going wild around the rink, they're also going wild into the stands. It's a funny thing. The other day, I was at a school talking with a few hundred kids. One kid came up to me and said, "Mr. Maniago, I'd like to ask you why you flinch whenever Bobby Hull shoots the puck?" I looked at the kid and said, "I'd like to ask you what you would do if Bobby Hull was shooting at you?" and he didn't answer. I don't care which goalie goes in there—when Bobby Hull winds up and hits the puck, that goalie is automatically going to flinch. The way Hull shoots, a flinch is the only human response.

The Year Bobby Cracked the Golden Fifty

Game	Goal	Date (1965–66)	Opposition Game Score	Opposition Goalie
1	1–3	Oct. 23	Chi. 4 at Tor. 0	Bower
2	4	Oct. 24	Chi. 6 at Bos. 2	Johnston
3	5–6	Oct. 28	Chi. 5 at Det. 1	Crozier
4	7–8	Oct. 30	Chi. 6 at Mtl. 4	Worsley, Hodge
6	9–11	Nov. 7	Tor. 0 at Chi. 6	Sawchuk
8	12	Nov. 13	Mtl. 5 at Chi. 2	Worsley
10	13–14	Nov. 17	Chi. 5 at N.Y. 3	Giacomin
11	15	Nov. 20	Chi. 1 at Tor. 3	Sawchuk
18	16	Dec. 4	Chi. 10 at Bos. 1	Parent
19	17	Dec. 5	Chi. 6 at N.Y. 2	Giacomin
23	18–21	Dec. 15	Bos. 4 at Chi. 8	Cheevers
25	22–23	Dec. 19	Det. 4 at Chi. 2	Crozier
26	24–25	Dec. 22	N.Y. 3 at Chi. 4	Simmons
27	26–27	Dec. 25	Chi. 3 at Tor. 5	Sawchuk
30	28	Dec. 31	Chi. 4 at Det. 1	Crozier
31	29	Jan. 2	Bos. 1 at Chi. 3	Johnston
32	30–31	Jan. 5	Chi. 4 at Mtl. 2	Worsley
34	32	Jan. 9	Tor. 3 at Chi. 5	Sawchuk
37	33–36	Jan. 16	N.Y. 6 at Chi. 5	Maniago
38	37	Jan. 20	Chi. 3 at Bos. 4	Johnston
40	38	Jan. 23	Mtl. 3 at Chi. 3	Worsley
41	39	Jan. 26	Chi. 4 at Mtl. 2	Hodge
42	40	Jan. 27	Chi. 3 at Bos. 5	Johnston

The Year Bobby Cracked the Golden Fifty (Cont'd)

Game	Goal	*Date* *(1965–66)*	*Opposition* *Game Score*	*Opposition* *Goalie*
43	41–42	Jan. 29	Det. 4 at Chi. 4	Crozier
45	43–44	Feb. 2	N.Y. 3 at Chi. 4	Giacomin
49	45	Feb. 12	Mtl. 2 at Chi. 2	Worsley
51	46	Feb. 16	Chi. 5 at N.Y. 2	Giacomin
53	47	Feb. 20	Bos. 1 at Chi. 5	Johnston
55	48	Feb. 26	Chi. 4 at Det. 1	Crozier
56	49	Feb. 27	Bos. 1 at Chi. 7	Parent
57	50	Mar. 2	Det. 4 at Chi. 5	Bassen
61	51	Mar. 12	N.Y. 2 at Chi. 4	Maniago

SHORT SHOT

According to Wren Blair, general manager and coach of the Minnesota North Stars, the St. Louis Blues organist, Norm Kramer, is worth at least one goal a game.

One night, during the 1968 Stanley Cup playoffs, the Blues were trailing the North Stars 3–0.

Since the Blues seemed to be playing like a team that just didn't give a damn, Lynn Patrick, their managing director, sent a note up to organist Kramer to play "When the Saints Go Marching In" (a tune Kramer had renamed "When the Blues Go Marching In"). Lynn felt that the tune might give the team a lift.

But even he never expected what happened. Before Kramer had gotten through two choruses, the pepped-up Blues had poured five goals past Minnesota's Cesare Maniago and skated off with a 5–3 victory.

After the game, Blair flipped out. "We didn't get beat by a hockey team," he roared. "We got beat by a God damned organist."

5

The Policemen: Enforcers on Ice

Every team has a policeman. He is the heavy—the fighter. The guy who protects his teammates from the bullies on the opposing teams.

Ted Green has the job in Boston, Reggie Fleming in Philadelphia, John Ferguson in Montreal, while Orland Kurtenbach does the job in New York.

Some policemen, like Ferguson, Green and Fleming, never back away from fights—they sometimes even go looking for them—while others, like Ted Harris and Orland Kurtenbach, mind their own business until trouble actually breaks out somewhere on the ice.

To most NHL fans, Ted Green of the Bruins is the epitome of the bad guy. And he epitomized the epitome one night during the 1968–69 season when he broke the record for penalties in one game and had the Rangers' president, Bill Jennings, issuing a reward for Green's scalp before the night was over.

It all happened on December 26, 1968, when Ted, who'd missed 14 games because of a virus, returned to the ice in Madison Square Garden with fire in his eyes.

Though Ted threw his weight around for all of the first, and part of the second, period, the Rangers held a commanding lead, and the New York fans were really giving Ted the business about his dirty play.

But the jeers turned to threats on his life when, midway through the second period, Teddy went into the Ranger corner after the puck. He thought he saw one of the Ranger defensemen coming at him, so at the last minute he stuck out the butt end of his stick.

Green's stick dug into the stomach of Ranger Phil Goyette, who was coming over only to tie up the puck. Goyette went down like a sack of potatoes, and the Rangers had lost their star center for the balance of the season.

During the remainder of the game, the incensed Ranger patrons threw papers, coins, cups, beer cans—and everything else they could get their hands on—at Green. He was finally banished from the game in the third period when he tangled with Vic Hadfield. His total penalties for the night were three minors, two majors and two misconducts—a record that experts say will stand for a long time.

"Of course, I wasn't trying to hurt him," said Green after the game, in his own defense. "Goyette is one of the cleanest players in the league. I certainly wouldn't purposely try to injure him. When I went into the corner,

I was expecting to get hit and I was just turning around to defend myself. I never even saw Goyette."

Ted's explanation failed to soothe the Ranger management. President Bill Jennings, who was all but flipped out with anger, shouted, "When a wild animal is loose, a bounty is put on his head. So I'm offering a bounty for Green."

Naturally Jennings spoke out of anger; he later rescinded his remarks.

Just before the opening of the 1969–70 season, Ted got into a stick-swinging duel with Wayne Maki of the St. Louis Blues and suffered a fractured skull. As of this writing, it is not known whether Ted will ever play hockey again.

One of his teammates, however, who probably knows Ted better than anyone else, had this to say: "A fractured skull won't keep a tough guy like Green out of action. He'll be back before the end of the season with a steel plate in his head."

Reggie Fleming, another player who would rather fight than score, has already played with four of the six original NHL teams and is now with Philadelphia in the expansion league.

Fleming came up with the Canadiens but, shortly after, was traded to the Chicago Black Hawks. There he played slam-bang hockey until Chicago coach Billy Reay soured on him when he drew a rather foolish two-minute penalty for charging in the last three minutes of the seventh game of the 1963–64 semifinals against Detroit. With Fleming in the jug, the Hawks were unable to mount an attack and succumbed to the fourth-place Wings.

"That does it," said Reay. "Head hunting is all right but in its time and place."

The following year found Reggie in Boston. In the middle of the season, coach Milt Schmidt decided that Reggie wasn't hustling enough and packed him off to the Rangers.

And with the Rangers, Reggie, the policeman, came into his own.

He led the league in penalties in 1965–66, spending 166 minutes in the box.

In the early part of the 1967–68 season, Reggie had one of his better nights. It was halfway through the second period, and the Toronto Maple Leafs were giving the Rangers hell on ice.

Suddenly, Ranger coach Emile Francis turned to Reggie and said, "Get in there, Reg, and let's see what you can stir up."

Fleming jumped over the boards and immediately sent Maple Leaf forward Ron Ellis spinning with a crushing body check. Moments later, referee Art Skov detected Fleming in the act of charging and sent him to the sin bin for two minutes.

After serving his time, Fleming made a couple of quick sorties to the Toronto goal. As he cut in front of John Bower, the elderly cage custodian for the Maple Leafs cut Reggie's skates out from under him. Although Reg did not have the puck at the time and was merely maneuvering for position, he bounced up like a bull and charged referee Skov, all the while yelling for a penalty against Bower. When Skov said no, Reg charged the referee and deliberately smashed him to the ice with a cross check. Everyone watching thought for sure that Skov would toss Fleming out of the game and fine him.

For some unknown reason, however, Skov did not penalize Fleming and started play again from the face-off circle to the right of the Toronto net. As soon as the puck dropped, Reginald dropped a pair of Maple Leafs, Duane Rupp and Pete Stenkowski, against the 50th Street side boards and completely took them out of play.

In the confusion, Orland Kurtenbach picked up the puck, passed it to Harry Howell, took a return relay from Arnie Brown and flipped it past Bower for the tying goal. Bobby Nevin later won the game for the Rangers in the third period with a 55 footer.

In the press room after the game, Francis gave Fleming complete credit for turning the game around: "He was hitting everyone in sight out there. He completely confused them. They were worrying about Fleming instead of the puck. Reggie has this talent. Sometimes he even confuses us."

Well, let's hope Reggie doesn't confuse the Rangers too much any more, because he's now playing for the Philadelphia Flyers.

John Ferguson, the policeman of the Montreal Canadiens, is a dark and brooding character, who is decidedly mean while on the ice—a man not to be trifled with in any circumstances. In the dressing room before a game, he gets into his uniform quietly, eyeing even his teammates coldly, and then sits unsmiling in his corner until it's time to go out on the ice. He does not make conversation. He does not go in for backslapping or handshaking. This man has no friends, and when the team gets the signal to go out on the ice, his attitude is already bordering on the hostile.

Scarcely will the game be underway before John Ferguson will be dealing out shattering body checks to any who cross his path. If they retaliate, he'll belt them with his stick or, if circumstances warrant, batter them senseless with his fists. He's a man who's ready to hit back even before he's hit.

In the 1968–69 season, Ferguson was number three on Hockey's Bad Boy list, with 185 minutes in the penalty box.

Jean Beliveau, team captain of the Montreal Canadiens, had this to say about Ferguson: "In today's hockey, you need a man like Ferguson to act as a kind of policeman. But he's more than that, really, because he's a good hockey player. After all, he is a potential 20-goal-a-year man. Other teams have policemen too, but they only score maybe five or six goals a season. So Ferguson helps his team in two ways—by scoring and by making the opposition keep their heads up."

Certainly hockey has its enforcers, and they are around to keep the peace, but as one Hockey Hall of Famer put it to this writer while standing at the Picadilly Bar in Montreal's Mount Royal Hotel: "There is no such thing as a real tough guy in hockey because no matter how tall or broad or muscled or rough a guy may be, the other fellow always has the equalizer—his stick."

SHORT SHOT

In the early days of the game, teams carried only one or two substitutes and it was not unusual for a player to go out onto the ice and stay there for a full game. Frank (King) Clancy, now assistant manager of the Maple Leafs, recalls a game in which the team's only relief defenseman was too sick to dress. It was a busy night for Clancy with plenty of action, puck-carrying and digging. "Halfway through the last period, I could hardly stand," he remembers. "My lungs were bursting and my arms and legs were numb with fatigue."

Clancy signaled the bench that he wanted to come out. The team had a spare forward, and Clancy figured that he could play defense for a short time—but the coach shook his head. Clancy was to stay in the game.

So Clancy did the only thing he could do. The next time an opposing player got close enough to him, Clancy tripped him up with his stick, got a tripping penalty and a well-deserved two-minute rest.

6

Gordie Howe: He Has Been Called the Greatest of Them All

When a veteran hockey writer was asked to name three All-Star teams, past, present and future, his answer was, "Start with Gordie Howe, put him on all three."

There is no arguing with that statement, for Gordie Howe is truly of the past, present and future.

Gordie Howe, the powerful right-winger for the Detroit Red Wings, holds virtually every career record in the books. He holds the all-time record for most goals scored, for most assists, for most points, for most games played. He has been named the National Hockey League's Most Valuable Player a record six times and has won the scoring championship six times. Altogether, Howe holds more than a dozen league records. But probably the one he enjoys most is the one for longevity.

In 1965–66, he tied the 20-year record set by Boston's Dit Clapper and the next season he broke it. And each season after that—1967–68, 1968–69—he broke his own record. Considering that the average hockey player lasts

6.6 years in the NHL, playing 24 seasons is truly an amazing feat.

When asked if he'll try for 25, Howe smiles and says, "Well, the hours are good and the pay is excellent."

To achieve what Howe has achieved requires real virtuosity. "The thing you've got to know about Howe," said a player from a rival team, "is that he can do everything better than anybody else." He is, in short, the greatest hockey player who has ever come down the pike.

At the end of the 1968–69 season, Howe had 732 goals to his credit, but when asked which of those goals he remembers best, his answer is his first and his last. One he does discuss rather fondly is the goal he got the night Jim Norris promised him a watch if he scored. He put the puck in the nets only once that night, but it was enough to earn him a $240 watch—and he did it the hard way. Late in the third period he took the puck down ice, shot from about 20 feet out, fell head over heels and was flat on his back when the red light went on.

The most satisfying goal of Gordie's whole career, however, came during the 1963–64 season.

In the latter part of October, Howe had tied Maurice Richard's all-time scoring record with his 544th goal. It was November 11, 1963, the Red Wings were playing at home against the Montreal Canadiens and goalie Charlie Hodge, who had shut Gordie out the previous Saturday. And he was doing it again. Through the first and most of the second period, Howe had been limited to three shots and each of them had been tossed aside by Charlie Hodge.

Late in the second period, with Detroit leading 2–0, Alex Faulkner—new to the Wings—slashed Ralph Backstrom of the Canadiens and drew a five-minute penalty. Sid Abel, the Detroit coach, motioned Howe and Billy McNeill to take the ice to kill the penalty.

Play resumed. The Canadiens sent the puck deep. It bounced off the end board and stopped dead behind the Detroit goal. Defenseman Marcel Pronovost picked it up and sent a pass to Howe, moving up the ice. Howe immediately fired to McNeill, who brought it over the Montreal blue line. McNeill then passed the puck back to Howe. Thirty feet from the net Gordie took it. It was a wrist shot.

"I knew it was in when I let it go," Howe said afterward.

But probably Howe remembers best the goals he didn't score.

Late one season, Red Kelly, a Detroit defenseman, took a shot at the net. Gordie, who was near the net, deflected the puck and sent it into the twines. Kelly was going for a record 20 goals for a defenseman at the time, and when it was announced that he'd gotten credit for the goal, Kelly told Howe he knew better. But Howe said, forget it, who needs one more or less goal, he'd get more before the season was over. Howe did get more, but he fell just one short of 50, which then was the record. With that goal, he could have made it.

Another goal that Howe didn't get, and another he probably remembers vividly, happened during the 1952–53 season. In a game against the Rangers, Howe took a shot from 20 feet out and Lorne (Gump) Worsley deflected it. But in so doing, he fell flat on his face on the ice. Howe charged in. The puck was lying loose right in front of Gump's face. Many a player would have slashed the puck and all but decapitated Worsley. But not Howe. He dashed in, protected the puck from the other players and held it long enough for Gump to reach out and smother it. When Worsley got to his feet, he looked at Howe and muttered, "Thanks, bud."

Howe shrugged. "Forget it," he said. "I'll still get a few goals off you and you'll still stop a few of my shots, so consider us even."

Another year in which Gordie Howe fell one short of that magic number 50 was 1952–53.

When asked why he goes on playing hockey, he answers coolly and simply: "I keep playing because I like the game. Every game is a new challenge. But every game is pain, too. You learn to live with pain. I suppose I'll play until the legs give out. I've seen it happen to others. The legs hurt so bad you can't go on. Sid Abel won the Most Valuable Player Award one year, and the next year, his legs went. At the end of the season, he said his legs ached so bad he couldn't sleep and he was going to quit. The boss said to see how he felt by fall. In the fall, the legs still hurt. He was done. Bill Gadsby, Red Kelly, they went until the legs hurt them too much.

"Right now, my legs hurt occasionally. I fool around in practice because after all what good is this if you can't have fun at it, and then we have a hard practice and suddenly there's nothing there, and I know I'm tired, but that's all it is so far, just tired. I have more bad games than I used to. But that's all, so far. I'm not as good as I was, but the stats are holding up. When the time comes, I'm not so proud I won't struggle through one more season, but I'll quit if I think I'm cheating the team or the fans of what they're paying for."

One thing you can bet is that Gordie Howe, probably the greatest hockey player who has ever lived, won't cheat anybody.

Right now, he's earning $75,000 a year. And when we say earning, we mean exactly that. He earns every penny the Detroit Red Wings pay him. He's probably worth twice that amount.

SHORT SHOT

Terrence Reardon, brilliant defenseman for the Montreal Canadiens, once received five penalties in one game against the Rangers. The following day was his birthday. He received a telegram of congratulations from his sister. It was addressed:

Terrence Reardon
Penalty Box
Montreal, Canada

7

The Ten Greatest Hockey Teams

The Montreal Canadiens of 1955–56—the greatest team ever to hit the ice.

Who says so?

Hockey managers, coaches, players, writers and broadcasters. And they said so in October, 1969, in a poll taken by *Hockey World* magazine.

The 1955–56 Montreal aggregation beat out the 1951–52 Red Wings by two voting points and the 1950–51 Boston Bruins by three points. In fourth place were the Toronto Maple Leafs of 1947–48; fifth, the 1928 New York Rangers, with the Boston Bruins of 1929–30 in sixth place, followed by the 1931–32 Montreal Canadiens.

Rounding out the top ten—the 1926–27 Ottawa Senators, the 1943–44 Canadiens, and, finally, the 1966–67 Chicago Black Hawks.

1955–56 was Hector (Toe) Blake's first year as coach of the Montreal Canadiens, and that year they took it all. For a rookie coach, Toe Blake manipulated the Canadiens like a veteran. He had invited 54 men to training camp and retained three rookies—Henri Richard, Claude Provost and Jean Guy Talbot. Blake got Butch Bouchard, who had announced his retirement, to stay on as Captain. By mid-February, the Canadiens had virtually clinched the NHL championship.

When the season ended, the Canadiens held the NHL championship with 100 points and took most of the individual awards.

Jean Beliveau won the Hart Trophy as the league's most valuable player; he also won the scoring title with 47 goals and 41 assists for a total of 88 points. Maurice Richard was second-highest scorer with 38; Geoffrion came in third with 29. Jacques Plante won the first of five straight Vezina Trophies allowing only 1.86 goals per game. Doug Harvey, Plante and Beliveau made the first All-Star hockey team, while Tom Johnson and Bert Olmstead made the second team.

The Canadiens scored a record 222 goals that season and also permitted the fewest to be scored against them —only 131.

Other hockey greats on that great team included Dickie Moore, Bob Turner, Dollard St. Laurent, Butch Bouchard, Ken Mosdell, Don Marshall and Jackie Leclair.

In the playoffs, the Canadiens lost only one game to the Rangers in the semifinals. They outscored them 24–9 on the series; they lost only one game to Detroit in the finals, outscoring the Red Wings 18–9.

Jean Beliveau scored the opening goal in what proved

to be the final game, giving him 59 goals on the year, including the playoffs.

From 1956, the Canadiens went on to win five straight Stanley Cups and six out of seven pennants.

They were truly the greatest, even though some still consider the 1951–52 Detroit Red Wings the classiest bunch of guys ever to lace on a pair of skates.

The Red Wings put together one of the best won-lost records ever—winning 44, losing only 14 and tying 12.

Goalie Terry Sawchuk won the Vezina Trophy, allowing only 1.90 goals per game and turning 12 shutouts. Gordie Howe was voted the league's most valuable player in 1951–52 and also won the scoring title with 43 goals and 43 assists for a total of 86 points.

Red Kelly paced a solid defense, scoring 17 goals himself and assisting on 37 others, while Ted Lindsay took care of the "policeman" duties.

Sawchuk, Kelly, Lindsay and Howe all made the All-Star first team. Other star performers on that team were Marcel Pronovost, Tony Leswick, Metro Prystai, Marty Pavelich, Glen Skov, Alex Delvecchio, Vic Stasiuk, Johnny Wilson, Bob Goldham, Leo Reise, Ben Woit and Larry Zeidel.

After ripping the league apart during the season, the 1951–52 Detroit Red Wings became the first team in history to sweep the Stanley Cup in just eight games—four of them shutouts.

The 1940–41 Boston Bruins also have to be considered one of the top teams in the hockey world.

In going for their fourth straight pennant, the Bruins established two records that year. Between December 22, 1940, and March 13, 1941, they went 15 games without a loss, tying six and winning nine for the longest home stand without a defeat. (This was later tied by Detroit in 1941.) Additionally, between December 22, 1940, and February 25, 1941, they went 23 games without a defeat, winning 15 and tying 8. The Rangers stopped the streak in Boston by beating the Bruins 2–0.

In the Stanley Cup games, Boston beat Toronto 4–3, and then went on to sweep Detroit, 4–0.

Bill Cowley won the Most Valuable Player Award and the scoring title, getting 17 goals and setting up 45 others.

The team's offense also was sparked by the "Kraut Line" of Milt Schmidt, Woody Dumart and Bobby Bauer. Roy Conacher, Eddie Wiseman and Art Jackson contributed to a balanced offense.

Dit Clapper, who later became one of the first 20-year men in the NHL, anchored the defense while Frankie (Mr. Zero) Brimsek manned the nets. Cowley and Clapper made the first All-Star team, while Brimsek, Bauer and Dumart made the second.

Others on that fine club were Des Smith, Flash Hollett, Johnny Crawford, Pat McCreavy, Herb Cain, Mel Hill, Terry Reardon and Jack Shewchuk.

The 1947–48 Toronto Maple Leafs also came in for their share of glory. And it was probably a deal swung by Conn Smythe late in October that put them on the threshold of greatness. Realizing that he needed strength

John Bucyk of Boson takes puck past
Montreal defenseman Gilles Tremblay.

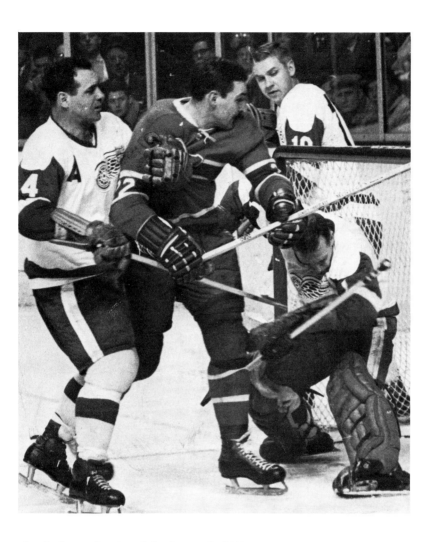

Goalie Roger Crozier of the Detroit Red Wings
is konked by Montreal left-winger John Ferguson
as Detroit center Alex Delvecchio looks on from
rear. Defenseman Leo Boivin (4) is also there.

New York Rangers' defenseman Arnie Brown is pinned
on boards by Montreal center Ralph Backstrom.

Boston's Bobby Orr is checked by Maple Leaf
defenseman Allan Stanley after getting off a shot.

Montreal Canadien Tremblay (3), with teammate
Jacques Lemaire following, takes puck past
Pete Stemkowski of the Detroit Red Wings.

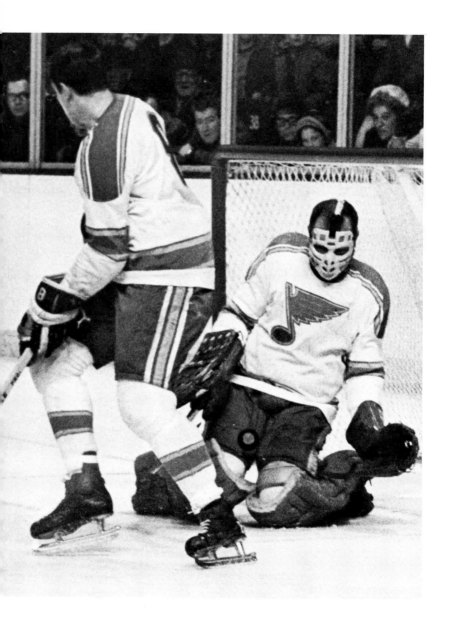

St. Louis Blues' goalie Glenn Hall (in mask)
and teammate defenseman Barclay Plager
figure two sticks are better than one when
it comes to keeping the puck out of the nets.

Jean Ratelle of the Rangers tries to check
Montreal's Gilles Tremblay (5) as he scores
on New York's goalie Ed Giacomin. Puck is
in upper-left-hand corner of net. Also around
goal are Rangers Brad Park (2) and Jim Neil-
son (15). No. 25 is Montreal's Jacques Lemaire.

down the middle, Conn sent Gus Bodnar, Ernie Dickens, Gaye Stewart, Bud Poile and Bob Goldham to Chicago in return for Max Bentley, the league scoring champion, and the then unknown Cy Thomas. It was one of the biggest deals ever swung in the NHL and went a long way to emphasize the worth of such a player as Bentley.

With the strength they needed, the Leafs proceeded to win the pennant and then beat Boston, four out of five, and Detroit, four straight, to win the Stanley Cup.

Turk Broda was the backbone of the club. The big goalie won the Vezina Trophy with a 2.38 goals-against average, then compiled a 2.22 figure in the playoffs. Bill Barilko and Gus Mortson were the badmen of the brutal defense, while Max Bentley proved his worth by leading the Leafs with 26 goals and 28 assists for 54 points. Syl Apps, who had come out of retirement that year, also had 26 goals, and Ted Kennedy wound up with 25.

Others on this great team were Jim Thomson, Wally Stanowski, Garth Boesch, Phil Samis, Don and Nick Metz, Vic Lynn, Howie Meeker, Joe Klukay, Les Costello and Sid Smith.

Without a doubt, the 1927–28 New York Rangers was one of the most dramatic hockey teams ever assembled. Coached and managed by Lester Patrick, the team was edged out of the pennant by Boston over a 44-game schedule but went on to nose out Pittsburgh and Boston in the first two rounds of the playoffs. Then the Rangers beat the Montreal Maroons three games to two to win the Stanley Cup. The second game of the finals against the

Maroons saw Les Patrick himself, at the age of 45, taking over the goaltending duties and allowing but one goal during the second and third periods. (This feat is covered more thoroughly in Chapter 11.)

Frank Boucher was the top scorer for the Rangers that year with 23 goals. Bill and Bun Cook filled out the front line, while Ching Johnson and Lorne Chabot braced the defense.

The 1929 Boston Bruins lost only 13 games while winning 26 and tying five during the regular season. They then went on to beat the Canadiens three straight and the Rangers two straight to win the Stanley Cup. They won the pennant again in 1930 with a 38–5–1 record but were upset by the Canadiens in the playoffs.

The violent Eddie Shore was the star of this team, while Harry Oliver, Dutch Gainor and Cooney Weiland provided the offense punch. Lionel Hitchman, Dit Clapper and Perk Galbraith took care of the defense.

The Montreal Canadiens took all the marbles in 1932. Leo Dandurand managed the club. Cecil Hart was the coach. Howie Morenz was the star of the team, while Aurel Joliat, Johnny Gagnon, Pit Lebine and Nick Wasnie also did heavy duty. The great George Hainsworth played goalie. Memorable performers also included Syl and George Mantha, Battleship Leduc and Armand Mondou.

The 1927 Ottawa Senators compiled a 30–10–4 record for the regular season and then swept the playoffs without a defeat. Offensively, Cy Denneny took the laurels, while the great King Clancy and Hooley Smith provided the punch.

Hec Kilrea, Frank Finnigan, Frank Nighbor, George Boucher and Jack Adams were also members of this club. Alex Connell, one of the game's great net minders gave up only four goals in six playoff games.

It's hard to say why a team like the 1944 Montreal Canadiens wound up ninth place in the ratings; it boasted some of the greatest athletes hockey has ever seen. Maurice The Rocket Richard scored 32 goals. Gerry Heffernan and Ray Getliffe came in with 28 apiece. Toe Blake picked up 26, while Elmer Lach put 24 into the nets. Murph Chamberlain and Fern Majeau played brilliant defense. The muscle was added by Butch Bouchard and Mike McMahon. One of the greatest goalies of all time, Bill Durnan, played in the nets and won his first of four straight Vezina Trophies. (He won six in seven seasons.)

The following season, Maurice Richard scored 50 goals (a record until Bobby Hull came along), and Elmer Lach won the scoring title with 80 points, but the team was upset in the playoffs by the Toronto Maple Leafs.

The 1967 Chicago Black Hawks did things no other team ever did before them. They scored 264 goals, a record at that time. Stan Mikita won the scoring championship with 35 goals, 62 assists and an NHL record-tying 97 points. Bobby Hull scored 52 goals, more in one season than anyone else in 50 years of the NHL.

Stan Mikita was named the most valuable player in the

The Greatest Teams in Hockey History

Rank	Year	Team	Manager	Coach	Stars
1	1956	Montreal Canadiens	Selke	Blake	Beliveau, Richard, Harvey
2	1952	Detroit Red Wings	Adams	Ivan	Howe, Kelly, Sawchuk
3	1941	Boston Bruins	Ross	Weiland	Cowley, Clapper, Brimsek
4	1948	Toronto Maple Leafs	Smythe	Day	Kennedy Apps, Broda
5	1928	New York Rangers	Patrick	Patrick	Boucher, Cook, Johnson
6	1929	Boston Bruins	Ross	Ross	Shore, Weiland, Thompson
7	1932	Montreal Canadiens	Hart	Hart	Morenz, Joliat, Mantha
8	1927	Ottawa Senators	Gill	Gill	Denneny, Clancy, Connell
9	1944	Montreal Canadiens	Gorman	Irvin	Richard, Lach, Durnan
10	1967	Chicago Black Hawks	Ivan	Reay	Hull, Mikita, Pilote

league that season, and Bobby Hull, Ken Wharram and Pierre Pilote all made the first All-Star team, while goaltender Glenn Hall, with a goal-against average of 2.38, made the second team.

But with all of this going for them, Billy Reay's 1967 Chicago Black Hawks did not win the Stanley Cup that year. Punch Imlach's Toronto Maple Leafs upset them. And maybe because of this, this team, which had just about everything, came in tenth in 1968–69 instead of in the first five.

Of course, it's hard to compare teams like the 1927 Ottawa Senators, the 1967 Chicago Black Hawks and the 1944 Montreal Canadiens. Times change, playing conditions change, rules change, and only the experts can take everything into consideration.

SHORT SHOT

. . . Mervyn (Red) Dutton, from NHL exile to NHL president.

In the beginning of the 1942–43 season, the NHL board of governors knew that the New York Americans' lease was about to expire at Madison Square Garden and also knew that the team that was always a weak sister would be even weaker after losing quite a few players to Uncle Sam. It therefore decided that the team should resign from the NHL for the good of the league.

Red Dutton, owner of the Americans, who had just been kicked out of the game he loved, retained reserve rights to all of his players and vowed he would be back in the league with a team when the war ended.

He was back faster than he thought—but not with a new team.

In January, 1943, Frank Calder, head of the league, had a heart attack and died.

Red Dutton, who had been kicked out of the league just a few months earlier, was approached to take over for Frank Calder. When it was found that he would take the job, the same owners who had kicked him out voted unanimously to bring him back—as president.

8

Bobby Orr: The NHL's First Bonus Baby

Leading football and baseball and basketball players have been picking up huge bonuses to sign contracts for some time now. Namath received $400,000 to sign with the New York Jets. Lou Alcindor got close to a million to sign with Minneapolis. But never in the history of hockey had anyone received a bonus of any sizable amount to sign a contract. The greatest of them all, Gordie Howe, received $4,000 and a Red Wing jacket to sign with Detroit.

Bobby Orr, star defenseman for the Boston Bruins, changed all that. Working through a Toronto attorney, R. Alan Eagleson, Bobby Orr received between $50,000 and $100,000 to sign a Boston contract.

Eagleson wouldn't disclose the precise terms but affirmed that the money was much closer to $100,000 than to $50,000—and added that, besides the money, Orr has the option of going to college, should he choose to, on the Boston Bruins.

But even if Boston had paid Orr $1 million, he would have been worth it.

"Only one great hockey player comes along every ten or twenty years," said Harry Howell, ex-New York Ranger, now with the Oakland Seals, "and Bobby Orr is that man for these ten years." Howell went on to call the Boston defenseman a star's star.

Bobby Orr, a square-jawed, crew-cut young bull, is a proven great at only 22 years of age. Orr's poise, his moves and his electrifying style of play won him rookie-of-the-year honors in 1966 and the Norris Memorial Trophy as the league's outstanding defense player of 1968–69.

Also during the '68–69 season, Bobby became the first defenseman in 24 years to score over 20 goals—he got 21. One night he even turned the hat trick in Boston and some 75 hats were thrown onto the ice. "Too bad I've never worn a hat," Bobby said.

Boston fans already regard Orr as the greatest find since Ted Williams or Carl Yastrzemski or Bob Cousy or Bill Russell. And the exception that proves the rule is a leather-voiced, dyed-in-the-wool hockey fan who yells to Bobby from the Boston Garden's third balcony, "Hey, Orr, why don't you play defense for a change?"

Boston Globe sportswriter Will McDonagh summed up Bobby best when he said: "Bobby's appeal is what they all dream about—a kid starring in the big leagues. Carl Yastrzemski of the Boston Red Sox is a batting champion who is real big with the small fry, but Yaz is like a businessman. He has been around for a while, he's had his ups

80

and downs and now he finally has made it. But this kid, Orr, is just that, a kid."

If one has to compare Orr with any other big leaguer, it has to be Willie Mays—who used to patrol center field for the New York Giants during the afternoon and then in the evening play stickball with the kids in Harlem. Those who played with him say he was better than a three-sewer hitter.

Orr loves hockey the way Mays loves baseball. When both were only rookies, it was apparent to anyone connected with sports that they would be great. They would be stars—one day, probably, be members of the all-time All-Stars in their own fields.

In 1966, his first year with the Bruins, Orr quickly became the leader. "As soon as the players get on the ice, right away they're looking for Orr," said a player with an opposing team. Shouts from his teammates to "Take it, Bobby, take it," were frequent. And Bobby took it. Although in his rookie season—and he missed 9 games because of a knee injury—he still lit up the goal light 13 times and tossed teammates 28 assists, for a total of 41 points. When Gordie Howe broke in with Detroit, he scored 7 goals and gave off 15 assists for 22 points. Bobby Hull, as a rookie with Chicago, poked in 13 goals and had 34 assists for 47 points. But the most important part of these statistics is the fact that both Bobby Hull and Gordie Howe were forwards, not defensemen, Orr is a *defenseman*.

When Bobby Orr starts away on one of his rink-length

dashes, it is really a spectacle. Orr starts behind his own net. If the opposition forechecks closely, he will weave his way through the traffic. Otherwise, he charges out and moves either straight up center ice or down the right wing. He is a sure stickhandler who can control the puck at his fastest speed. "When he goes by my bench," says Punch Imlach, ex-Toronto coach, "I turn away so I won't have to watch."

Past the blue line, it's up to Bobby what he does with the puck. He can either pass off to a teammate or take it all the way himself, and through his natural hockey sense, the 22-year-old invariably makes the right decision.

When he takes it in himself, the fans flip; when he lights the little red light, it's pandemonium. You'd think the Boston Garden was filled with teenagers and the Beatles had just walked on. Bobby has a low, line-drive shot from the blue line, and he's as accurate as Sargeant York when he aims for the corners. In fact, that low-spinning shot of Bobby's comes in so fast that when a goalie is successful in stopping it, Bobby's teammates have a good shot at a rebound.

Despite the accolades and the star status thrust on him at such a young age, Bobby remains a level-headed young man. As far as he is concerned, his press clippings are for the fans to read, not him. "I try to ignore what the newspapers and magazines say," he once stated. "I'm so afraid of getting a swelled head, I rarely read the stuff."

Orr is a fighter. There is no room in his vocabulary for the word "lose." And because of his intense desire to win, he frequently gets into scrapes on the ice. He has had so many brawls he has become one of the better fighters in the game. He was tested by virtually all of the league's policemen in his rookie year and won more decisions than he lost.

"I never had a fight before I came to Boston," Orr said in an interview. "Some people think fighting is terrible, but I think the odd scrap—without sticks—is part of the game."

Bobby believes in getting in the first punch in a fight and then, while the man is momentarily stunned, throwing his haymaker.

He has a standing feud with Reggie Fleming and is firmly convinced that Ted Harris of the Canadiens hates him. "We've been at it a few times, nothing serious, really, just the usual," Orr said. "I don't know what will happen next."

Althcugh Bobby has been around the big leagues for only four years, hockey experts like King Clancy of the Maple Leafs are already comparing him to Eddie Shore and Doug Harvey, the greatest defensemen in the annals of the NHL.

"I think Orr is a ringer for Eddie Shore when Eddie first broke into the NHL," says Clancy. "Bobby isn't as old or as heavy-set as Eddie was when he came from the Western wheat fields, but he has the same kind of poise out there. He skates like Shore, moves the puck the same way—head up, looking for a teammate to pass off to, or an opening to sprint for. I think Orr will be just as great as Shore before he finishes his career. When he's on the ice, the Bruins look like a hockey team; without him, they are nothing.

"Shore was one of the greatest defensemen of his era, and Doug Harvey of his," Clancy went on. "However, it took Harvey almost ten years to get the savvy that Orr showed from his first game. Right now, I would still take Shore over Orr, but Bobby may surpass him eventually. Shore had one weakness that Orr does not have. You could get the better of his temper and goad him into stupid penalties."

But with all this success, Orr is still a nice guy off the ice. On the ice he has become a scrapper—he has to be. There are a lot of guys in the NHL who'd rather have Orr on the bench than on defense.

"Some of the older guys took runs at me when I was a rookie," says Bobby, "and I had to show them I could dish it out as well as take it. Now I fight only if I think it will help the team."

Bobby Orr, the so-called perfect hockey machine, does have one flaw: his gimpy knees. If they hold up, there's no telling how far Orr will go.

Harry Sinden, the Boston coach, has this to say about Bobby and his injury-prone knees, which have kept him out of a number of games: "Bobby hasn't yet learned to pace himself. When he does, he will play a few seasons in a row without missing too many games. Right now, he tries to carry the team on his back by himself at times. Naturally, he gets hurt.

Bobby Orr

"Every coach has to have a guy like Bobby if he really hopes to win at all. When things start to break down on the ice, you look along the bench and wonder what you can do to change the momentum. All I have to say is 'Bob, get out there,' and suddenly the whole flow of the game is new."

But no matter whether he's fighting, checking forwards or making his own rush toward the opposing goal, Orr is tops in the NHL. And maybe Harry Howell, ex-New York Ranger defenseman who won the James Norris Memorial Trophy as the league's outstanding defenseman in 1967, summed up Bobby Orr best when he accepted that award. "I've been around for fifteen years," said Harry, "and thank God, I finally won the trophy. I've got a feeling that for the next 20 years it will be known as the Bobby Orr Trophy."

SHORT SHOT

It isn't often a player has the last word with a referee, but Nick Metz, a Toronto forward, had just that in a game in the early '40s.

Seems that Nick, who was usually a very quiet guy on the ice, was doing a lot of complaining about the way Bill Chadwick was refereeing the game. Finally, Chadwick exploded. "Look, Nick," he yelled. "I'll referee this game. Your job is to put that little round black thing into that great big net. So get to it."

Soon after that, Metz scored. As he skated back to his position, he passed Chadwick and cracked, "You know, Bill, your job is to referee this game. You're not supposed to coach us players."

9

The Year They Rewrote the Record Book

In 1968–69 they rewrote the record book in the NHL.

Bobby Hull scored 58 goals, more than any single player had ever scored before. Phil Esposito of the Bruins came up with more assists—77—and more points—126—than were scored by any one player since the inception of the NHL. Gordie Howe had more assists—59—and more points—103—than any right-winger in the NHL history, and Bobby Hull had more goals and more points than any left-winger ever scored.

Bobby Orr came up with 21 goals, more than any defenseman ever made, and more points, 64. Pat Stapleton, with 50 assists, broke the record for defensemen in that department.

The play of two great lines also upended the record book. As a unit, Detroit's trio—right-winger Gordie Howe, center Alex Delvecchio and left-winger Frankie Mahovlich—scored 114 goals, surpassing the previous high of 105 set by Maurice Richard, Elmer Lach and Toe Blake of the 1944–45 Canadiens. Mahovlich scored 48 goals, Howe 42, and Delvecchio shoved 24 pucks into the nets. When the Montreal line set the record, Richard had 50 goals, Blake 29 and Lach 26.

Another great line—Boston's right-winger Ken Hodge, center Phil Esposito and left-winger Ron Murphy—totaled 263 scoring points to break the record of 226 held by the 1956–57 Detroit Red Wings' line of Howe, Norm Ullman and Ted Lindsay. To shatter that mark, Esposito came up with 123 points on 48 goals and 75 assists, Hodge made 88 points on 45 goals and 43 assists and Murphy scored 52 points on 16 goals and 36 assists. Previously, Gordie Howe had had 89 points, Lindsay 85 and Ullman 52.

The Boston Bruins, with 303 goals and 497 assists, totaling 800 points, broke every existing team-scoring record.

Among other scoring records tied were four goals in one period and six goals in a game by Red Berenson of St. Louis. Bobby Hull also tied the record of scoring in ten consecutive games. Pat Stapleton tied a record for defensemen with six assists in one game. Brad Park and Walt Tkaczuk of New York tied the record of four assists in one game by a rookie, and Danny Grant of Minnesota and Norm Ferguson of Oakland tied the rookie scoring record with 34 goals.

Finally, it was the first time in the history of the game that six men scored over 40 goals in one season. Hull had 58, Mahovlich and Esposito had 49 each, Hodge poked in 45, Howe came up with 44 and Yvan Cournoyer of Montreal scored 43. And, probably the most significant statistic of all, Gordie Howe—playing in his 23rd season at the age of 41—had his greatest scoring season ever.

SHORT SHOT

In one of the strangest fines ever levied on a hockey team, each player of the Los Angeles Kings was assessed $100 by owner Jack Kent Cooke. They were fined not for getting into an argument with a referee but for *not* getting into an argument with a referee.

On January 1, 1969, the Kings played a scoreless tie with the St. Louis Blues. Jack Kent Cooke, however, did not think it was a scoreless tie.

In the third period, Bill Flett, right-winger for the Kings, slapped a shot at Jacques Plante that went right by him, hit the goal posts, bounced around some and then flew back onto the playing area.

It seemed to have been in the net. Even referee Ron Wicks was sufficiently unsure to skate over to question the goal judge, Ken Watson. But not one of the Los Angeles Kings protested. They just finished out the "scoreless" game.

Later, in the locker room, owner Jack Kent Cooke told the players he had never been so ashamed of a team in his life. He said he could not understand their lack of interest, and on the spot fined every one of them $100— for *not* arguing with the referee.

91

10

Jean Beliveau

Jean Beliveau, All-Star center for the Montreal Canadiens, has played 16 seasons in the NHL and has com-
peted in 16 straight Stanley Cup playoffs—a record which
is going to be mighty hard to beat.

During those 16 seasons, Jean, the rangy center who
has been labeled *le Gros Bill*—the Big Boy—by the Montreal fans, has scored 463 goals in regular season league
competition (fourth on the all-time scoring list) and 73
red-lighters in Stanley Cup playoffs.

But of all the pucks he has belted into the twines, Jean
remembers two of them most vividly.

It was April 10, 1956. Montreal was playing Detroit at
the Forum, and Jean Beliveau went into that game with
11 goals, one short of the record held by his teammate
Maurice Richard for most goals scored in a playoff year.
The Rocket had set the record in 1944, with 12 goals
against Toronto and Chicago.

As the game got underway, it became apparent that
goals were going to be hard to get. The contest developed

into a goalie's duel between Montreal's Jacques Plante and Detroit's Glenn Hall. (Oddly enough, these same two goalies played with St. Louis in 1968–69 and together won the Vezina Trophy.)

There was no score during the first period, and halfway through the second period the score still remained 0–0. Then Red Wing defenseman Marcel Pronovost got a penalty. Montreal's first power play led by Jean Beliveau was broken up by Gordie Howe, who dumped the puck back into the Canadiens' zone. Doug Harvey retrieved it and slid a pass to Floyd Curry on the right. Curry just missed a check, then zoomed for the Detroit end of the rink, with Beliveau racing up to join him. Down the ice they went. Then Beliveau took a pass from Curry, cut in sharply on Glenn Hall and whipped a neat backhander past the lunging Detroit goalie. It was 1–0 for the Canadiens and goal 12 for Beliveau. He had tied the Rocket's long-standing playoff record.

Early in the third period, Beliveau got his last chance to break the record. Going in with Boom Boom Geoffrion, he ripped a shot that Hall got his glove on. The rebound came out in front of the net and the Boomer drove it past Hall.

The other goal that was most important in Beliveau's most impressive career happened on December 22, 1963. Montreal was playing Detroit at Olympia Stadium in Detroit. Late in the first period, Beliveau took a pass from Bobby Rousseau about 20 feet in front of the Red Wings' goal, then shot. It was a high hard slap to the left of goalie Roger Crozier. Crozier made a violent stab at it with his gloved hand, but he was caught out of position and the puck cut into the net. The red light flashed. It was Jean Beliveau's 325th career goal, and it established an all-time record for centers—a record that still stands.

Jean Beliveau has been a star most of his life. At just 17, he was the best known and most widely acclaimed junior player in Canada's history. Three years later, he was an outstanding forward with the Quebec Aces and had more press clippings as an amateur than the average player collects in a lifetime.

Montreal, who had an option on his services, made him many offers, but the big center rejected every one of them. He had no intention of turning pro. He was tops in his league and was making a substantial income from outside interests during hockey's off season.

Finally, the Canadiens came up with an offer that Beliveau just couldn't turn down—$100,000 for five seasons. Frank Selke, manager of the Montreal team, said the offer was "the highest ever given any player, the highest by a city block."

That year, when he reported to the Montreal training camp, one newspaperman wrote: "Beliveau will have to turn out to be a combination of Maurice Richard, Gordie Howe and Howie Morenz or else he'll be a flop."

And in his first season, Beliveau was exactly that—a flop. Hampered by injuries, he played in only 44 out of 70 games, scored an unimpressive 13 goals and came up with 21 assists. It looked as if the Canadiens had bought themselves a $100,000 lemon.

The following year, Beliveau began to come into his own. He didn't miss a game, put 37 pucks past opposing goalies and set up 36 more for a total of 73 points, just two points shy of the league leader, teammate Boom Boom Geoffrion.

And in the 15 subsequent years, Beliveau has proved that not only is he not a lemon; he's a $1 million package with a 100-grand price tag. Today, Beliveau rates with Howie Morenz as one of the greatest centers in hockey history. He can do everything. He's fast on the blades both forward and backward. He's a stalwart on defense; he can pass; he can backcheck. He's an outstanding playmaker, and he shoots with uncanny accuracy. As one of his teammates put it: "Unless you've played hockey, it's impossible to recognize the difficult things Beliveau can do. And he does everything well and effortlessly. What he does, he does better than anyone else who does it."

During his first two seasons in the league, Beliveau took one helluva beating from everyone. He was high-sticked, hooked, tripped and kicked. Even little guys would take a shot at him because they knew he'd never retaliate. He got the reputation of a pacifist.

But in his third year, Beliveau served notice on the league early in the season that he was no longer going to be a patsy. In a game against Toronto, he got into a ferocious high-sticking affair with George Armstrong. Both were given penalties. But that didn't stop them. They continued their skirmish even after the referee had given the order for them to leave the ice. Finally, they were both sent to the showers. That was Jean Beliveau's first fight, but it wasn't the last. At the season's end, Beliveau was near the top of the list in minutes spent in the penalty box.

Probably the greatest compliment ever paid Beliveau came from a Toronto player who prefers to remain nameless. He said, "When we need a game and we're ahead by one goal, the guy I most hate to see with the puck is Jean Beliveau. He can do anything with it—set up a play or rap it into the net. He's the greatest in the clutch."

And that's what hockey is all about. Anyone who has even a passing interest in the game must surely know that the playoffs are the proving ground for the giants of the game. Unless a man can deliver for his team under relentless pressure, he will never achieve true greatness in the league. Many a player or coach has been cast off by his team because he let them down when the going was rough. Those who survive the pressure-cooker conditions of playoff hockey are sure of a place of honor.

Beliveau has always come through.

Jean is now reaping the rewards of his greatness. He is the president of Jean Beliveau, Incorporated, and as such he gets paid for smoking a particular brand of cigarettes, for driving a certain car, for using a particular brand of shaving cream.

"I'm not going to be a millionaire," Beliveau says. "I do not ever expect to be a millionaire, but there are opportunities now which we did not have only a few years ago. One thing I know for sure, if there is a lot of money to be made and kept, it must be made while I am still playing. Nobody is anxious to go after someone who no longer is playing," he adds.

Just three short years ago, Jean had a completely different attitude. At that time he said, "I am at an age when I can no longer hope to go higher than third place in goal scoring. I cannot catch the Rocket and I surely cannot catch Howe. I have no real wish to do so. I never really thought I could score as many as 300 goals in the NHL and now I will be very pleased to score 400 [at the end of the 1968–69 season, he has scored 463], but at my age these things are not too important. To know that I have done my best is important."

Many times, Jean Beliveau has thought of retiring from the game. And he probably came closest to it back in 1966, when the Canadiens were playing Chicago at the Forum in Montreal.

He was moving down the ice toward the Chicago goal when someone brought a stick high and stuck it right in Jean's eye. The pain hit him like a bolt of lightning, and he slumped to the ice like a dead man.

As he lay there, all but unconscious from the excruciating pain, his only thought was, would he ever be able to see again.

"To tell you the truth," he says of the incident, "I was not worried about who did it [he never did find out]. I was more nervous than anything. The pain did not really bother me. The first thing I did—it is natural, I suppose—was open my eye to see if the vision was there. I could not even see the bright lights."

For four days he lay in a hospital bed without moving. He was told that any sort of exertion, any movement could cost him the sight of his eye.

Finally, he recovered. "I still think about that eye injury," he says. "Nothing is worth my eyesight. Nothing in the world."

Then he adds, "I have reached the age, I do not fool myself, where another serious injury would be the end. But when we get older, we have to take care of ourselves more. That is not to say that we do not play as hard as we can. Maybe, though, we are a little smarter after so many years in the league. In more ways than one—and maybe because we are a little smarter—we score a little more when it counts."

And when it counts, Beliveau has probably scored as many goals as any player past or present. Along these lines, it is interesting to note that only two players have scored two Stanley Cup winning goals for their team since 1927. Toe Blake, forward and ex-coach for Montreal, is one—Jean Beliveau, the other.

The French press in Montreal calls Beliveau *Le Prince Royal du Hockey*—a name that certainly needs no translation to anyone who ever saw him play.

SHORT SHOT

For some reason, early hockey pucks were made in two halves and cemented together.

In a game back around 1872, a slick skating forward fired a shot toward his opponent's goal. In its flight, the two halves of the puck separated. One half flew into the corner of the rink but the other half flew into the goal.

Was it a score?

Naturally the defenders said, "No!" Just as naturally the attackers yelled, "Yes!"

The referee had never had to make a call like this before, but, cool as a cucumber, he pulled the rule book from his pocket, read a little, closed the pages and returned them to his pocket.

"No goal," he said.

The attackers kicked up a fuss, but the ref remained adamant. "The rules say a puck must be one inch thick. The object that went into the goal was only half an inch thick. Therefore, it can't be a legal puck, and without a legal puck, you can't score a legal goal."

11

Two Successful Comebacks—and One
That Fizzled

Lester Patrick, who carved a legend in the NHL, had long since retired from the game and was coaching the New York Rangers in the finals of the 1928 Stanley Cup playoffs.

Midway through the second period of the final game with the Montreal Maroons, Lorne Chabot, the Ranger goalkeeper, was hit smack in the eye with a puck off the stick of Nels Stewart of the Maroons. He was knocked cold.

As a team in those days carried only one goalie, Les Patrick asked Eddie Gerard, the Maroon's manager, if he could use Alex Connell, the great Ottawa goalie, who happened to be a spectator that night, in the nets.

Gerard refused.

Les then asked permission to use Hugh McCormick, the goalie for London in the Canadian Pro League, who was also in the stands.

Permission again was refused.

Realizing he was getting nowhere, Patrick decided to quit asking and act.

He put on Lorne Chabot's pads, donned a pair of skates and played in the net himself. At the time, Patrick was 45 years old. He had never played goalie in his life—but throughout the rest of the game and on through the over-time, Patrick allowed but one goal.

The Rangers won the game and went on to win the Stanley Cup.

Twenty-five years later, Lynn Patrick, Lester's son, was coaching for the Boston Bruins as they played the Cana-diens for the Stanley Cup.

Patrick's goalie, Sugar Jim Henry, suffered a crippling leg injury and had to leave the ice. To make matters worse, Henry's replacement—(for many years now hockey teams have carried two goalies) was gashed by a skate blade and forced to leave the ice for medical attention.

While the goalie was being stitched, young Patrick grumbled and groaned. A Boston sportswriter reminded Lynn of what his father had done in a similar situation.

"Why don't you take over as goalie?" the writer asked. "It would make a great story. A 'like father, like son' yarn."

"Are you crazy?" Patrick asked. "I'd get killed!"

"I guess your generation must be softer," the writer challenged.

"Yeah," Patrick flipped back, "but not in the head!"

Another player who made a great comeback in one of the toughest sports in the world was tough Ted Lindsay, who ended a four-year retirement in 1964 when he decided to play another year for the Red Wings so he could officially end his playing career where he began it—in Detroit. When he had retired in 1960, he'd been a member of the Chicago Black Hawks.

As a Red Winger, it didn't take long for him to get back into the old familiar groove. He picked up his feud with Dickie Moore of the Maple Leafs right where he'd dropped it four years before, got himself into a few knock-down-drag-out battles with Ted Harris of the Canadiens (lost most of them) and harassed league officials in every arena in which he played.

In midseason, the 40-year-old left-winger got into a verbal battle with referee Vern Buffey and was assessed a misconduct penalty and finally thrown out of the game. He turned down a private hearing with the league president, to which he was entitled, but mouthed off to members of the press about the league president's kangaroo court.

That action called for a written apology and a $75 fine.

With 14 goals and 14 assists and 173 minutes in the penalty box in 69 games, Ted Lindsay had truly made a comeback.

From the 1923–24 season to the 1933–34 season, Howarth (Howie) Morenz of the Montreal Canadiens was one of the best centers in the history of the game.

There are those who will tell you he was and still is *the* best.

For 10 years he averaged more than 20 goals a season, and this at a time of 40- and 44-game schedules.

He could defend, and he could pass. And when it came to skating, an opponent once remarked, "When Howie skates at full speed, all the rest of us seem to be skating backward."

But after the 1932–33 season, Morenz's speed seemed to fade. His shots were no longer accurate. His body checking left a lot to be desired.

In the 1933–34 season, Morenz went into a tailspin, and so did the Canadiens. Howie scored only eight goals, and before the season was over a new player, Pit Lepine, had taken his place in the line.

When Howie did play, he heard boos for the first time in his life.

Before the season was over, Howie was traded to Chicago, then to New York. He did neither team any good and finally decided to retire.

But then in 1936, a new group of owners acquired the Montreal Canadiens, and the first thing they did was to bring Howie back.

Back in the Forum, Morenz caught fire. He seemed to have regained his matchless skills, and once again he heard the crowd cheer his flashing speed and breakneck dashes down the ice.

Howie was ablaze on the comeback trail.

Then on the night of January 28, 1937, in a game against the Black Hawks, tragedy struck.

Midway through the first period, Howie charged the

goal. He was checked by a Chicago defenseman. His skate caught in a rut in the ice. He careened off the boards and went down hard.

He tried to get up, but couldn't. His left leg and ankle were broken.

"I'm through," he gasped as he was being taken to the hospital. "I'm all through!"

After that, there was talk of another comeback for the gutsy little Howie—but it never came off. Morenz seemed to know it wouldn't.

Early in February, 1937, Morenz suffered a nervous breakdown. He died on March 8.

Doctors said that he died of an embolism. Those who knew him best said he died of a broken heart.

On March 10, 1937, 25,000 fans filed past his coffin at center ice in the Montreal Forum.

SHORT SHOT

One of the roughest hockey games ever played was a contest between Ottawa and Kenora back in 1906. Bodies took a tremendous hammering. The ice was red with blood.

Near the end of the game, one Kenora player was tripped by a rushing Ottawa forward. He fell on his head and slid in front of his own goal. He had trouble getting up. The referee saw him, but instead of lending a helping hand, the ref assessed the player a five-minute penalty for, of all things, obstructing his own goal.

12

Eddie Shore: The Edmonton Express

"I'll tell you what's wrong with Eddie Shore," said Eddie Shore in an interview. "He's always been in the wrong. He doesn't mean to be but he gets in people's bad graces. . . ."

And maybe the above quote explains why Shore, four-time winner of the Hart Trophy, annually awarded to the player in the NHL considered the most valuable to his club, and seven-time choice for the NHL All-Star team, was passed over when the charter members of the Hall of Fame were announced in 1947.

Of course, this oversight was rectified the following year; because of public outcry, Shore's name was selected in 1948. But the fact remains that Eddie Shore, who many hockey buffs claim was the greatest player the game has ever known, certainly the best defenseman, was passed over by the hockey "establishment" and will never have the satisfaction of seeing his name on the list of charter members.

Eddie Shore was a loner. A man with an incredible temper who spent most of his time on the ice committing hockey crimes that he later sincerely regretted, he was continually "getting even" with someone and didn't care how much punishment he took as long as he inflicted just a little bit more.

As Elmer Ferguson, a great hockey writer once observed: Eddie Shore "gave no quarter and he asked none. One night in 1929, the Montreal Maroons deliberately set upon him. A long-reaching jab with a stick-blade tore open his cheek. Another sliced his chin. He was hammered, pounded, cut, and just at the end, a Maroon player cut across Shore and deliberately gave him a sickening smash in the mouth which knocked out several teeth and felled Eddie in his tracks. He was carried off, and five minutes later, his wounds temporarily doctored, he was silently standing beneath the showers. Expecting an outburst, I said, 'Rough going, Eddie.' Through bloody, swollen lips, he answered, laconically, 'It's all in the game. I'll pay off.' "

Shore was a slow starter. He was all of 22 when he turned pro with the Regina Caps in the Western Canada League. The next season he played with Edmonton, and he looked so good that when the Western Canada League was disbanded, just about every team in the NHL tried to buy him early rather than take a chance on pulling his name from a hat. Boston was lucky.

Eddie Shore

As for Shore, who was to become known as "the fight-ingest guy in hockey," he got right off into the first of his many NHL battles—the only difference being that this one just happened to be with one of his own teammates.

Billy Coutu was Shore's adversary. He was the Bruins' star defenseman at the time Eddie Shore came up, and he didn't take kindly to any guy trying to take his job away from him.

Coutu was rough, and he was tough. He tipped the scales at 200 and the tape measure at just over six feet. And for two days he and Eddie pounded each other un-mercifully in practice. Finally, on the third day, Coutu picked up a puck behind his own goal and started up the ice. He may have been heading for the opposite goal, but his target was Shore. Eddie wasn't about to give any ground.

They met literally head to head at center ice. Coutu reeled from the impact and fell unconscious onto the ice. Shore remained standing, but his left ear was split from top to bottom.

From that day on, Eddie was the first string defense-man for the Bruins.

However, Eddie still got off to a slow start. He played his first game in the Boston Garden on November 16, 1926, and did absolutely nothing. But he must have shown some spark, since the next day a sportswriter for the *Boston Transcript* had this to say: "Eddie Shore caught the fancy of the fans. The new defenseman is tall and sturdily built. His speed is exceptional and he handles his body and his stick very well."

But if Eddie was a slow starter, he was an impressive finisher, because from the middle of the 1926–27 season through 1940, Shore was "Mr. Defense" in the NHL and brought to it a brand of rough-and-tumble that never has been equaled. He antagonized fans, fought opponents, harassed officials and kicked up more hell than any other man in the game before or since. Opponents often teamed up to cream him. Owners wanted to outlaw him, and fans came to games to do nothing but scream at him. But they came. For Eddie Shore, they came in droves.

Eddie Shore was fast, and he was reckless. He had no regard for his own safety, certainly even less for the safety of any other man on the ice. During his playing career, Eddie came close to killing one man, but many times he came close to being killed.

Once, in a game against the New York Americans, Shore was flying down the ice on one of his power rushes when he got checked and went down. He popped up immediately, but Rabbit McVeigh, who had been trailing the play, was just about on top of him. When Rabbit saw Shore's head come up from the ice, he jumped—but he didn't jump high enough. The tip of one of Rabbit's skates caught Eddie right between the eyes.

Blood spurted forth like a gusher. Many of the spectators thought Eddie was out of action for good. The shot did put him out of action, but only for one minute—the amount of time it took for Eddie to skate to the sidelines and stick a piece of tape over the gash.

Another time, in a game against the New York Rangers, Eddie collided with the goal post while traveling at a terrific speed. He was knocked out cold.

And he was still out cold in the dressing room when the Bruins left for Montreal, where they had a game the following night. Finally Shore was taken to the hospital, where an examination revealed that he had broken three ribs. The doctor ordered bed rest for at least a week—but later, when a nurse went in to give Eddie a pill, she found an empty bed. Shore had left for Montreal, where he played the next night with three broken ribs and scored two goals and assisted on another.

Because of Eddie's complete abandon, his jet-propelled speed and his powerful shot, when Boston came up with a scoring play, Shore, flanked by two speedy forwards, moved down the ice like a bulldozer. Eddie would take the puck down the ice from his own territory. When the enemy defense moved in to check, he would uncork a powerful shot, not toward the goal but toward the end-boards, and then streak down the ice after it. When the puck came careening off the boards, Eddie was there. He would retrieve the puck, pass it to one of the two forwards who were now moving into position, and very often the little red light would blink goal.

But although Eddie could do virtually everything with a stick and a puck, the strength of his game was defense, and he and his partner, Lionel Hitchman, handled that part of the game like nobody before them.

"Don't try and go outside," the word quickly spread around the league, "because they'll break your back on the boards. But also watch out when you're going inside, because Eddie and Lionel will make a sandwich out of you and probably leave you flat out on the ice."

Shore's body checks are legendary in the NHL. He hit like a Mack truck—and very often the guy he hit was so stunned and so mad, he'd retaliate with his fists or his stick—mostly his stick.

Shore usually managed to inflict more punishment than he received. One night, however, during the 1927–28 season, he got a little more than he gave. Blood streamed down his face as the game drew to a close. And just before the final minute, Babe Siebert of the Canadiens gave him a helluva wallop, right across the face with his stick. Eddie hit the ice and was unconscious for 15 minutes. After the game, it was found that Shore had a broken nose, three cracked teeth, both eyes blacked and a brain concussion from the wallop on the head. But this didn't stop Eddie; the next night he was back on the ice, just as nasty as ever.

It is unfortunate that Eddie is remembered mostly for his brawling instead of for his tremendous skating ability, his accurate shooting and his brilliant defense play. During his career, he scored 105 goals and made 178 assists—certainly not up among the scoring leaders; but then Eddie Shore was a guy who'd rather fight than score.

Eddie Shore

In 1940, his body battered and his big league career just about over, Shore put what money he had saved back into the game he loved and bought the Springfield team in the American Hockey League—the second strongest league in the game. And he was the most unusual owner-coach the sport has ever known.

"Call him wild, call him off-beat, call him a kook, call him a nut," said Emile Francis of the Rangers, "and whatever it is you call him, you'll probably be right."

"He can scare a guy just by looking at him and often does," says defenseman Don Johns, who played a year under Eddie's tutelage in Springfield, "but every hockey player should get a chance to play with Shore, just to know what the hell the game is all about. And if the player survives, he'll always have something to tell his grandchildren—although they may not believe it."

Johns also tells about the time he was immobilized in a hospital bed with a 40-stitch cut in his leg. The phone rang; it was Eddie. Before even asking Johns how he felt, Eddie said, "You ought to be able to play pretty soon," and hung up before Johns could say so much as a word. Johns was flabbergasted.

After a week, Johns was released from the hospital and reported back to the team. That night, Eddie put him in the game for three minutes and then suspended him for a week.

"When I played hockey," Eddie said, "I once had 100 stitches in my leg and I was out only three—no, two and a half days."

117

Shore managed the Springfield team, turning them into a hockey power second to none in the world, until 1967, when he retired. But he is still one of hockey's greatest fans.

"Most hockey players are a little crazy one way or another," Eddie Shore once said. "They have to be. Some of us admit it. As for me, I'm not sorry about anything I've done in my life. As long as I can be close to hockey, I'm happy to be alive."

SHORT SHOT

When Lord Stanley, who gave hockey the Stanley Cup, returned to England after his tenure as Governor General of Canada, he introduced the Canadian game of hockey to the British. One day, on the frozen lake in the grounds of Buckingham Palace, the five Stanley brothers, plus Lord Annally, played the Palace team. The latter group included the Prince of Wales (later King Edward VII), and the Duke of York (later King George V).

13

The St. Patrick's Day Riot

It was Sunday, March 13, 1955.

The Montreal Canadiens were playing the Boston Bruins at the Boston Garden. Always a hard-hitting team, the Bruins were giving the Canadiens a particularly rough time that night. At the end of the second period, Boston was ahead on goals and had inflicted an unusual amount of punishment on the Canadiens.

In between periods, Dick Irvin, the Montreal coach, gave his players a terrific tongue-lashing, and Maurice Richard went back to the ice sizzling with rage.

Then all hell broke loose. Hal Laycoe, veteran defenseman for the Bruins, swung his stick and, by his own admission, struck Richard on the head after feeling a sudden impact against his glasses. The blow on Richard's head opened a wound that required eight stitches to close. Partially stunned, and certainly angry as a bear, Maurice, spurting blood from his scalp, took off after Laycoe, who beat a hasty retreat. Laycoe's teammates and linesman Cliff Thompson tried to stop Richard, and, in the scuffle that followed, Maurice belted the official.

That was the spark that set off the St. Patrick's Day Riot—an explosion unprecedented in the annals of the NHL.

Between the spark and explosion was the hearing that was held in the office of Clarence Campbell, the league president.

Present were Maurice Richard, a bandage hiding his head wound; Hal Laycoe, with cuts about his face and a bandage over one eye; linesman Cliff Thompson, who was sporting a black eye; linesman Sammy Babcock; and referee Frank Udvari. Ken Reardon and Dick Irvin represented the Montreal Canadiens, and Lynn Patrick was there on behalf of the Bruins.

Hal Laycoe left at 12:35 P.M. to catch a plane to Boston to rejoin his teammates for a game against Detroit. The hearing ended an hour later.

The verdict: suspension of Maurice Richard for the remaining games of the season and for the Stanley Cup playoff games.

It was the severest decision ever handed down by Campbell since he had assumed office.

It was a particularly rough decision considering that Montreal was in first place, just barely ahead of Detroit in the standings—and also that Maurice Richard was on his way to his first scoring championship.

But according to Campbell's statement, Richard was not

suspended as much for the stick-swinging match with Laycoe as for striking linesman Cliff Thompson.

Ken Reardon, the only available spokesman for Montreal, said simply, "I'm stunned. Frank Selke and I will go over Campbell's statement letter by letter and see if any appeal will be made."

The following day, a few hours before a riot erupted in Montreal on account of the forfeiture of a scheduled game to the Red Wings, Frank Selke issued this statement:

> Although the club is surprised and annoyed at the decision, there would be no point in appealing Campbell's decision and presenting the case to the board of governors. It would be a case of clubs passing judgment on another club and that would be unfair to them and to the president of the league.

The defense taken by the Canadiens and presented in the press by Russ Wheatley, a veteran hockey writer, was a defense of stick-swinging, bludgeoning or punching officials. It was simply this:

1. That by Laycoe's own admission, he was the instigator of the brawl. He was quoted as saying, "I swung my stick and struck Richard after feeling a sudden impact against my glasses."

2. That the three officials who handled the game were confused and contradicted themselves in their statements.

3. That Richard, who was blinded by blood and half out of his head with anger, did not know he was hitting an official.

But the suspension stood. Richard would play no more that season.

The following day, Thursday, March 17, crowds began to assemble as early as midafternoon outside the Forum, carrying protest banners and demanding, "We want Campbell. . . . We want Campbell!" Had the crowd been dispersed then and there, and had the police maintained tighter control over the persons admitted to the Forum lobby, there wouldn't have been a riot later on—but who could foresee what was to happen?

That St. Patrick's Day game was one Montreal would never forget. Without Richard, the team just seemed to lie down and die. In no time at all, the Canadiens were behind by several goals, and the fans, stirred to boiling anger by Campbell's ruling, were in a dangerous mood.

Again came the shouts of "We want Campbell. . . . We want Campbell!"

And Campbell arrived at the hockey game in the middle of the first period with Detroit leading 2–0.

Shortly after Campbell seated himself, a disgruntled fan approached him with his hand extended in an apparent offer to shake hands. When Campbell reached to accept the outstretched hand, the fan pulled it back and punched him in the jaw. Then others joined in the punching and slapping of Campbell. Those who couldn't get near him threw rotten eggs, rotten tomatoes, bags full of water and, for some inexplicable reason, pickled pigs' feet. One young fan seized by the police was fined $25 "for squeezing a tomato on Mr. Campbell's head."

124

The St. Patrick's Day Riot

No sooner had the police surrounded Campbell than a tear-gas bomb exploded behind the south net.

The first period had ended, and the Red Wings, skating through a disorganized Montreal team, were leading 4–1.

When the gas bomb went off, people who had not left for intermission, scurried from their seats, half blinded and choking.

It was ascertained later that the bomb was actually thrown by a policeman; it probably saved Campbell's life. Instead of rushing the league president, the people rushed out of the arena.

The fire commissioner ordered the building cleared, and the game was forfeited to Detroit, putting them in first place.

Outside the Forum, the crowd regathered. Screams and shouts filled the air. A rifle shot slammed through the arena's windows.

The mob swept down St. Catherine Street, damaging cars, burning newsstands, wrecking phone booths, looting stores and stoning innocent people in street cars.

President Campbell barely escaped with his life.

He did not, however, rescind Richard's suspension.

SHORT SHOT

Even among the amateurs, hockey is a violent game.

In a contest between St. John and Twin Rivers in the Ottawa Valley League, one of the St. John forwards picked up a free puck off the boards. There were no players between him and the goal, and, while entertaining the thought of how he would describe this score to his wife when he got home, he started for the Twin Rivers net.

He never got there.

A minute later, he recovered consciousness with his teammates bending over him.

A little old lady, sitting along the rail, seeing the threat to her home team, had struck him on the head with her big, black handbag. The handle broke, and the contents spilled out onto the ice: three one-pound jars of cold cream. Obviously, this nice little old lady had come armed with a secret weapon—no miserable enemy breakaway was going to get past her along the boards.

14

Hall and Plante: The Grand Old Men of the Blues

When Scotty Bowman, coach of the St. Louis Blues, picked up Jacques Plante, 40 years old, as back-up goaltender for Glenn Hall, 38, in the beginning of the 1968–69 season, a lot of coaches, players and sportswriters laughed up their sleeves.

But Scotty had the last laugh.

Dividing the season pretty evenly, Hall and Plante became one of the greatest goal-minding duos in hockey history.

1. They won the Vezina Trophy, which is given to the team allowing the least goals scored against it.

2. They shared the distinction of being chosen as the outstanding performers in the NHL's Western Division. (It's rare for two men to be chosen; usually the award goes to one man.)

3. Glenn Hall became the first man from an expansion team to be chosen for the NHL All-Star team.

4. Their expert work between the pipes brought St. Louis into the finals of the Stanley Cup play.

Both were equally brilliant. Hall participated in 41 games, Plante appeared in 37, and between them they compiled an awesome 2.07 goaling average and finished 39 goals ahead of their nearest rivals. Hall and Plante racked up 13 shutouts along the way (a new team record) and pocketed $1,250 in bonus money for winning the Vezina Trophy.

Certainly goalies Hall and Plante were no laughing matter—except maybe for the St. Louis Blues. But stopping pucks is about the only thing Jacques Plante and Glenn Hall have in common. Whereas Hall hates the job and the game and plays it only for the money involved, Jacques loves it.

"I sometimes ask myself what the hell am I doing out here?" Hall said on one occasion. "But it's the only way I can support my family. If I could do it some other way, I wouldn't be playing goal."

While he was in retirement because of his wife's illness, Plante had this to say about one of the toughest jobs in sports: "I love the job. Goaltending was my life and I miss it so much. I would like to play again but I'm afraid it is impossible."

But Plante's wife is well again, and Plante is back in the game he loves.

Although Plante loves the game, he has always been a maverick. As Frank Selke of the Canadiens said when he traded Plante to the Rangers: "We got rid of Plante because we couldn't depend on him anymore. Worsley [the goalie they got in place of Plante] never saw the day he could play like Plante when Jacques was at his best—but Plante always had some new theory to try out. Toe Blake couldn't have taken much more without punching him in the nose. He's no team man. He's the best goalie I've ever had and close to the best I've ever seen—but that doesn't say he can run the hockey club."

Even Plante's first game in the NHL was far from routine. It was like a movie scenario. The Canadiens were down three games to two in the finals of the Stanley Cup playoff, with the sixth game coming up in Chicago. Dick Irvin, then coach of the Montreal team, decided it was time to change goalies, so Plante was called in to replace Gerry McNeil. And Plante did just that. He replaced McNeil, not only in the Stanley Cup playoff games, but also as first string goalie with the Canadiens. In his first game, Plante shut out the Black Hawks three to nothing, and two nights later the Canadiens won the Stanley Cup in Montreal.

For the next decade, Plante was the goalie on one of the finest teams in the history of hockey. But Plante did it his way. Up until the time Plante broke into the NHL, goalies never left the net. Plante decided a goalie could help his team by coming out of the net to clear the puck. It was a revolutionary idea, and his coaches told him not to do it. But Jacques did it anyway, and it proved so successful that today most goalies have adopted the technique.

Another innovation for which Jacques is responsible is the face mask.

On the night of November 2, 1959, Jacques, who was then playing goal for the Canadiens, was hit in the face by a puck fired by Andy Bathgate of the New York Rangers. Bleeding like a stuck pig, Jacques was removed to the Garden clinic, where seven stitches were taken in his nose. But seven stitches or no, Jacques had to return to the ice since teams carried only one goalie. And return Plante did, and when he did, the fans in Madison Square Garden let out a howl. The Montreal goalie was wearing a mask—the first mask ever worn in professional hockey. Toe Blake, coach of the Canadiens, was against it, vehemently against it. But Plante told him, "No mask, no play," so there was nothing Toe could do.

Plante had been experimenting with a special mask in practice sessions for five years. He had been cut for more than 200 stitches in his face, had his nose broken four times, both cheekbones broken and his skull fractured, yet any time he hinted that he might wear the mask in an actual game he was told not to. However, being Plante, he carried it with him.

The Canadiens won that night against the Rangers and kept right on winning for the next eighteen games, and Plante continued to wear the mask. And because the Canadiens went on to take all the marbles that year, no one ordered Jacques to remove the mask.

He has worn it ever since.

On the subject of his style of play and of wearing a

mask, Plante had this to say recently: "I don't say anyone should copy me, I do what works for me. It doesn't make sense to leave the net, but it makes less sense to let the puck go free. It doesn't make much sense to let your face hang out in the open to be cut to ribbons, but some guys aren't comfortable in masks, and the job comes first. Anyway you work it, it's a hard job for all us crazy guys and you have to be a little crazy to play goalie."

Even if Jacques Plante only introduced the face mask to professional hockey, he would deserve a place in the Hall of Fame. But in ten seasons with the Canadiens, two with the Rangers and one with the Blues, Plante proved to be one of the best goalies ever to pull on 40 pounds of padding. He has won the Vezina Trophy a total of seven times—a record. He was chosen for the All-Star team a total of three times, and in 1962 he became one of four goaltenders ever to win the Hart Trophy as the NHL's most valuable player.

Back in the 1950s, when Plante won the Vezina Trophy a total of five times in a row, his critics claimed that with a team as good as the Canadiens in front of them, even they could win the trophy. To this, Plante answered, "Doug Harvey is the greatest defenseman in hockey but he didn't win the Vezina, I did."

Right now, Plante is on a crusade against curved sticks. "It's just not right," he says. "It's too much—one of these days one [of] those crazy shots will kill one of us." If the past is any indication of the future, Plante will have his way. He always has had.

Just as much as Plante likes playing goalie, Glenn Hall hates it. In fact, no one who has ever played the position has ever come to hate it with quite the passion Glenn Hall displays.

Some 900 games and 33,000 shots ago, Hall was a pleasant young man who was proud to be a professional hockey player. Now, he's miserable. He hates the world and most of the people in it. He particularly hates hockey writers and hockey fans.

"I don't like people," Hall says, "I don't like to force myself to be a nice guy when I don't really want to be one. When I'm ugly, I'm really ugly."

There is practically nothing in the hockey world that can make Hall smile. Even his salary, which reportedly went as high as $60,000 in 1968–69, didn't please him that much. "It's little enough," he says, "considering what I have to do. There are four or five shots every game that hurt right through the pads and hurt for days afterward."

Like Plante, however, Hall is an innovator. Before Hall came along, playing goal was a stand-up job. Goalies just didn't leave their feet any more than they had to. Bill Durnan of the Canadiens in the 1940s was the epitome of the stand-up goaltender, and most up-and-coming goalies copied his style. Hall did not. His style of play was entirely new and different. In blocking shots, Hall spends as much time on his knees as he does on his feet. When he goes down, his knees spread out in a wide V, stretching almost from post to post. And while his legs protect against shots skimming along the ice, his gloved hand is

It looks so easy. Johnny Bower, Toronto Maple Leafs' goalie, picks a flying puck out of the air.

Montreal's great center Jean Beliveau (*left*)
is about to take puck away from Doug
Mohns, Chicago Black Hawks' right wing.

Chicago Black Hawk Bobby Hull gets set for slap shot.

Toronto Maple Leafs' right-winger Eddie Shack (23),
now with Los Angeles, cuts in on Boston goalie
Gerry Cheevers, fakes him out of position, and
slams puck into nets. Ted Green (rear) looks on.

Chicago's Bobby Hull with broken jaw returns
to action wearing helmet with face bars.

Montreal's right-winger Yvan Cournoyer (12) shoots; New York
Ranger goalie Ed Giacomin (1) stops puck with his belly.

Montreal Canadien defenseman Ted Harris pins
North Star center Wayne Connelly on boards.

Black Hawk defenseman Ken Wharram (rear) loses puck to
ex-Ranger great Boom Boom Geoffrion.

ready to catch any rising shots. By digging the toes of his skates into the ice, Hall can quickly bounce out of the crouch into a standing position to stop all high shots. This technique is particularly good against screened shots. "I can cover more ice this way," says Hall.

On the ice, Hall appears to have nerves of steel. But appearances, particularly that one, can be deceiving. Hall is probably the most uptight goalie ever to play in the NHL. Hall is actually physically sick before and even during most games in which he participates. And he has tried just about every cure there is for his nervous stomach. He even took tranquilizers, which helped his stomach but all but put him to sleep on the ice. And one thing a goalie doesn't want is to be half asleep. Even wide-awake, the net minder is hard pressed to escape with his life.

Despite the sickness and the nerves that precede every game, Glenn Hall has established one of the most remarkable records in the history of the sport. For six and a half seasons, Hall played in every one of his team's 70 games without missing a minute of steady action. During this streak, which stretched to 502 games, Hall was carried from the ice unconscious, sustained cuts that required up to thirty stitches at a time, yet always managed to stagger back onto the ice and finish the game. Considering these facts and considering that Hall is playing the toughest position in the sporting world, his record makes other endurance records pale by comparison.

Hall has won the Vezina Trophy three times and has been chosen for the NHL's All-Star team six times. But it was in the spring of 1961 when the Chicago Black Hawks won the Stanley Cup that Hall came up with the most brilliant performance of his career, possibly the greatest performance by a goalie in the history of the game. For 135 minutes and 26 seconds, Hall blanked a Canadien team that included on its roster such fine scorers as Boom Boom Geoffrion, Jean Beliveau and Henri Richard. And when Hall shut out the Montreal team in the Forum in Montreal on the night of April 1, 1961, it marked the first time the Canadiens had been blanked on their own ice in 88 consecutive games.

Hall has said he is ready to retire. But no one really takes this seriously. Hall has been saying that since he won the Calder Award for Rookie of the Year.

If he's serious about retiring, then the 40-year-old Plante will have to go it alone. But if Hall does play another year, then you can bet that the Plante-Hall combo, which is now probably as famous as the team of Rowan and Martin will again take the Blues into the Stanley Cup playoffs.

SHORT SHOT

One night in Chicago Stadium, the Black Hawks had the Montreal Canadiens down by one goal with only a few minutes left to be played in the third period.

Suddenly, out of nowhere, Rocket Richard scored two goals to snatch a victory for the Canadiens.

After the game, a Chicago sportswriter, who was usually on the baseball beat, asked Dick Irvin, then coach of the Black Hawks, "But why didn't you have someone prevent Richard from scoring those two goals?"

Irvin looked at him as though he thought him a complete idiot. "You're thinking of the wrong game," he said. "We can't walk the big hitters in hockey, you know. This game is played for keeps for 60 full minutes!"

15

The Ace Bailey Incident

It was December 12 of the 1933-34 season. That night the Toronto Maple Leafs were scheduled to play the Boston Bruins at the Garden in Boston.

At nine o'clock in the morning, the Toronto team detrained at Trinity Place, a small station near the University Club. And the first thing that caught their eye on the newsstand was a headline in the Boston morning papers: "I'M THROUGH PLAYING GENTLEMANLY HOCKEY: SHORE." The story went on to say that Eddie, after playing a hands-off type of gentlemanly hockey until then, had decided to return to the rough-and-tumble style which had established him as one of the most feared defensemen in the National Hockey League.

Now whether or not this was an accurate quote, no one really knows. But then, no one took his threat seriously anyway. Players frequently make startling statements just to give the hockey writers something to write about. Also, the fans had been on Eddie's back for his lackluster style of play over the first month or so. The statement, if Eddie made it, was certainly more to keep the fans off him than anything else.

That night, during the first period, the Leafs were out-playing Boston, but near the end of the period they were only one goal up when tempers flared. Before the excitement subsided, Andy Blair and Hap Day of the Leafs incurred penalties almost simultaneously. This caused coach Dick Irvin of Toronto to put in his penalty-killing unit of defensemen, Red Horner, King Clancy and one of the best men in the league when it came to ragging the puck to kill penalties, Irvin (Ace) Bailey.

After the face-off, Bailey got the puck, and for almost a full minute he dodged, twisted and squirmed, hanging onto the puck with the entire Boston team chasing him all over the ice. Finally the referee blew his whistle for a face-off, ruling that Bailey was not advancing the puck.

While time was out, Boston's coach, Art Ross, called Eddie Shore to his side. What he told him no one knows to this day, but it certainly had something to do with how to get that puck away from Bailey—for without it, Boston couldn't take advantage of Toronto's weakened condition.

Once again, on the face-off, Bailey came up with the puck. Again, he kept it for a time, but then he slammed the puck to the Bruins' end of the rink to give himself a breather.

Eddie Shore picked up the puck back of the Bruins' goal and started one of his spectacular rushes up the ice. But he didn't get far. As he went by, King Clancy, the Toronto defenseman, tapped Eddie on the front of his skates with his stick—an illegal move, but one seldom called by referees —sending Shore sprawling toward the boards.

140

The Ace Bailey Incident

Clancy took the puck and started for the Boston end of the ice. When Clancy started his rush, Shore made no attempt to rise. He stayed right there on his knees. He may have thought that a penalty would be called. He may have been trying to incur a penalty, or he may have been slowly losing his temper because no penalty had been called. Whatever it was, Bill Grimes, the referee, didn't help the situation when he told Eddie, "Get up, you farmer, nobody is paying any attention to you!"

Shore finally got to his feet behind Bailey who, from the exertion of the last few minutes, was bent over his blue line with the stick across his knees. Whether Shore mistook Bailey for Clancy, whether he just picked an enemy uniform or whether he was just so ticked-off at himself, the referee or hockey in general, nobody will ever know. But before anyone knew what was happening, the powerful Eddie Shore, sometimes referred to as "The Edmonton Express," worked up a full head of steam, caught Bailey from behind with his shoulder (some accounts say Shore used his stick to hook his victim) and flipped him high in the air. Bailey's head struck the ice with a sickening thud, and his body went limp.

Eddie Shore never looked back, he just kept going to his place at the blue line. A few in the crowd roared approval, but most people knew Bailey was badly hurt. He was lying on the blue line with his head turned sideways as though his neck were broken. His knees were raised, and his leg was twitching ominously. Suddenly the whole arena was quiet; now everyone knew that Bailey was badly hurt.

Red Horner, Bailey's teammate, skated over and tried to straighten Bailey's head, but it seemed locked in that grotesque position. Getting to his feet, he skated toward Eddie Shore. "Why the hell did you do that?" he screamed.

Eddie's lips formed a sickly smile, but Horner took Eddie's look to be that of a callous I-don't-give-a-damn-if-he-is-hurt smile. Horner was infuriated. He hit Shore with an uppercut, and Eddie hit the ice like a pole-axed steer. His head struck the ice and split open. In no time at all there was a halo of blood about Eddie's head.

This brought the Boston players from their bench. They advanced on Horner, who was now virtually alone on the ice—but before they could do any damage of their own, Charlie Conacher rushed to Horner's aid and as the two lifted their sticks to a fighting position, Conacher said to the approaching Boston brigade, "Which one of you is going to be the first one to get it?"

For some reason this challenge seemed to calm everyone down. And with the fight over, players rushed to the sides of the two unconscious hockey players.

Ace Bailey was carried into the dressing room. There, Dr. Kelly, the Boston Garden's official medico, looked at him and said, "If this boy is a Roman Catholic, we should call a priest right away."

Frank Selke, manager of the Leafs, told the doctor that Bailey was a Protestant. At that moment Bailey came to. "Put me back in the game," he pleaded. "They need me."

Bailey was rushed to the Audubon Hospital, where he

was found to have sustained a subdural hematoma, a blood clot that was causing a build-up of cerebral fluid. Twice, doctors despaired of his life. And twice his skull was opened up to relieve the pressure. He clung to life by a thread.

To complicate matters even further, Ace Bailey's father arrived in Boston with a gun, determined to shoot Eddie Shore on sight. Fast thinking by Frank Selke in this matter averted further tragedy.

Weeks went by. Newspapers carried daily bulletins on Bailey's progress. League officials added to the furor by becoming embroiled in a controversy over who was at fault, the game officials (who were accused of laxity) or the players. Shore was the target of most people's wrath and the league suspended him pending investigation.

Finally Bailey passed the crisis. He would live, but he would never play hockey again.

On February 14, 1934, the Toronto Maple Leafs staged an Ace Bailey night. The Leafs were to meet an NHL All-Star team—included on that team was Eddie Shore, the man Toronto fans had come to hate.

The players of the two teams were lined up on the blue line when Ace Bailey reached the face-off circle. Shore left his place in the line and skated over to where Ace Bailey stood. He put out his hand in a gesture of friendship. Bailey did not hesitate. He grasped Shore's hand, and the two men embraced each other.

The fans let out a roar of approval. Eddie Shore had

been forgiven by Ace Bailey—and the fans, who just a short while before were demanding that he be blacklisted from hockey for all time, forgave Shore, too.

Elmer Ferguson, hockey writer par excellence, reported next day in the *Montreal Herald:*

> There stood the two main actors in a drama that held a sports world breathless with suspense and fear for days as a gallant athlete fought for life with a tenacity and complete disregard for all the sinister medical precedents that amazed even the expert practitioners.
>
> The roaring crescendo of welcome struck its peak, of course, as the two clasped hands, but throughout the hockey battle that followed, as Shore played a typical, rushing, effective game, there was nothing but applause for his movements.
>
> It was a generous, fine and sporting episode in a sporting city's history.

SHORT SHOT

After 12 seasons in the NHL, Jacques Plante, a 36-year-old goalie with seven Vezina Trophy wins to his credit, decided to retire. (Of course, a year later he returned to hockey, to a new expansion team, the St. Louis Blues.)

At that time, a reporter asked Plante just what it was like to be a goaltender in the NHL.

Plante hesitated for a moment, then answered, "How would you like it," he asked, "if you were sitting in your office and made one little mistake? Suddenly, a big red light goes on and 18,000 people jump up *en masse* and start screaming at you, calling you a bum, an idiot and an imbecile. At times, they even throw garbage at you. That's what it's like to be a goaltender in the NHL."

16

Phil Esposito: What's He Gonna Do for an Encore?

In the 1968–69 season, Phil Esposito, All-Star center of the Boston Bruins, shattered the scoring record in the NHL. With 49 goals and 77 assists for a total of 126 points (the first man ever to go over 100 points in the NHL), Phil became the first Bruin to have his name inscribed on the Art Ross Trophy, which is awarded to the National Hockey League's individual scoring leader. (The last Boston player to win the scoring title was Herbie Cain in 1943–44, but that was four years before Art Ross donated the trophy bearing his name.)

Naturally, since then, every defenseman in the league has been keying on Phil.

But those defensemen know they have to come prepared, because although Esposito is pretty much of a pacifist at heart, he can get tough. And he got tough on February 8, 1969, when the Bruins were playing the Philadelphia Flyers in Boston. Midway through the second period, Phil and Philadelphia's Larry Hale got into a slashing brawl. Both were assessed penalties. But Esposito didn't think he deserved a penalty and let the referee know it in what might be termed blue language. The referee then slapped a "misconduct" on Esposito, which prompted Phil to haul off and belt the ref. For this display of "rowdyism," Phil was suspended for two games and fined $150. Many hockey observers figure this was a light sentence, considering the offense.

But whether Phil is belting referees or putting pucks past goalies, his main concern is his team, the Boston Bruins. Phil thinks of nothing but winning. "I'm not so much concerned about my individual record," he told a reporter after that 1968–69 year. "I'm excited about what our team can do. I'm out to win.

"You'll remember when I came to my first Boston camp two years ago, I set a kind of timetable. I was sure we'd make the playoffs in the first year, move up to third the second year, and win the Stanley Cup the third year. Well, we got ahead of that schedule by a year.

"And if we come up with the cup this year [he was talking of 1969–70], I don't care what my individual record may be. I still believe what I always did. You get eight points in a game and it doesn't mean a thing, if the team loses 9–8. It's a lot better even if you don't get any and the team wins 2–1."

Phil Esposito hates to lose. After the Bruins' Stanley Cup defeat by the Canadiens in a wild six-game set, Phil was really down. He blamed himself for what he considered missed opportunities, and he was aware of the muffled criticism and the innuendoes about his alleged inability to come through in the clutch.

As far as Phil was concerned, he agreed with his critics. For almost three months afterward, he brooded, playing and replaying those games in his mind. And after a thoroughly objective appraisal, he realized that he did all he could.

"After a while," he said, "I took another look and I let myself realize that I had more points than anybody else in the Stanley Cup series. Some of the time I must have been doing something right, eh?"

In 10 games, Esposito had 8 goals and 10 assists for 18 points. In 14 games, Montreal's Jean Beliveau had 5 goals and 10 assists for 15 points.

"When you shoot as much as I do, you have to think of the percentages," Phil went on, "and they weren't going for me all the time. Certainly I missed some that I should have made. Other times, I shot right at Rogatien Vachon [the Montreal goaltender] and don't forget that guy made some fantastic saves on me and the rest of our fellows. Let's give him some credit."

In giving Esposito their Player of the Year Award, the *Hockey News* said:

> There is little doubt that Esposito, with a record-smashing 126 points, 49 goals (a record for centers) and 77 assists (an NHL record) was the outstanding player of 1968–69.
>
> Esposito glittered in a highly productive NHL season in which records fell like tenpins in a bowling alley and he was the leader with men like Bobby Hull and Gordie Howe ex-

periencing remarkable seasons—only to be overshadowed by the rangy Boston center.

They may use names like Hull and Howe when talking of Phil Esposito, but they can't compare the Bruins' center with any player before him.

According to hockey writers, coaches, managers and goalies who've played against him, Esposito is like no other player past or present. He does not have the cold I'm-gonna-score-or-die-in-the-attempt intensity of Maurice Richard. He is not nearly as strong as Bobby Hull. His shots do not have the accuracy of Gordie Howe's. He is not as graceful as Jean Beliveau. Esposito has no style— he just scores. And so far, nobody has figured out how.

Esposito has no gimmick, although he himself realizes that to be a superstar you've got to be more than a super-scorer. To rise above the crowd like a Willie Mays, a Joe Namath, a Paul Hornung or a Sandy Koufax, you gotta have a gimmick. And because he hasn't, Phil Esposito remains, for all his exploits, much less of a star than his feats would indicate.

"I get more mail than I ever did before, since 1968–69," he says, "but I don't think I'll have to hire a secretary to answer it like Howe and Hull do. I don't even get much from people around my home town. I guess they figure they'll see me during the summer, so why write."

In his first two years with Boston, Esposito scored 210 points. Harry Sinden, coach of the Bruins, said recently,

Phil Esposito

"If Phil keeps going the way he's going, they're going to have to rewrite the record book.

"Phil's biggest virtue is patience," Sinden went on. "He'll skate around on the ice, hold the puck, wait until his man makes a move, never give the puck away under any circumstance. He just knows how to play. He may not be flashy—he just scores all the time."

In line with this, Emile Francis of the Rangers says that Esposito scores because he's big enough and strong enough to hang around the goal until the puck gets there.

"He's strong," says Francis, "and you can't get him away from the cage. All of a sudden, there's a loose puck and wham, he's got another goal."

Not many of Esposito's goals are long, clean, deliberate shots, but then very few of the goals scored during the entire NHL season are. Most goals are the result of pile-ups in front of the goal, traffic jams, busted plays with the goalie sprawled and the puck just sliding in past his outstretched glove or skate. These are the kinds of goals Esposito gets, but they count just as much as a beautiful slap shot from 25 feet out.

"They call me the 'garbage goal collector,'" says Phil, "but I don't care what they call me as long as the pucks go in."

Phil entered pro hockey in Sault Sainte Marie, his home town, in 1961. He was shipped to St. Louis in 1962, where he scored 90 points but was ignored by the NHL scouts.

"I quit that year and took a job driving a truck for my dad," says Phil, "but when an offer came to play for the Chicago Black Hawks, I grabbed it fast. Playing hockey sure beats pushing a truck."

In his first three seasons with the Black Hawks, Esposito —playing center and sometimes left wing—managed to score 55, 53 and 61 points, respectively. He also set up innumerable goals for Bobby Hull and Stan Mikita.

But Billy Reay, the coach, and Tommy Ivan, the general manager, felt that Phil's play left a lot to be desired. According to these men, Esposito was sloppy in practice, slow on defense and disappointing in Stanley Cup play.

So in 1967, the powers-that-be traded Phil Esposito to the Boston Bruins. And it is interesting to note that, after the trade, the Chicago team, which had always been one of the leaders, fell to the cellar in the NHL, and Boston, which had been a perennial cellar dweller, climbed to the top in the NHL.

Esposito didn't do it alone, but he certainly helped.

When the St. Louis Blues gave Red Berenson an automobile after scoring six goals in one game, Harold Kaese, a columnist for the *Boston Globe* said, "If Red Berenson's play is worth an auto to the St. Louis Blues, then the Bruins should give Esposito a gift of proportionate dimensions for what he has done for the team—say a Boeing 707."

SHORT SHOT

In 1958, Punch Imlach was hired as general manager and coach of the Toronto Maple Leafs. Before this job, he was known chiefly to his mother, his wife and a few inside hockey players.

The Leafs were in last place when he was hired, but in the final weeks of the 70-game league schedule they caught fire and, on the last night of the season, they beat Detroit in a game they had to win to reach fourth place and a berth in the Stanley Cup playoffs.

Sports pages and front pages alike called the Maple Leafs the Cinderella team. And though they did lose to Montreal in the finals, even this did not take away from the fact that Imlach had brought them out of the cellar into the daylight.

A few months after the season, Queen Elizabeth II visited Toronto, and Imlach, who could have passed unnoticed on any street the year before, was among the noted Canadians invited with their wives to lunch with the Queen.

Hockey alone had put him there—in less than a year.

17

You Gotta Be a Nut . . .

Someone once said, "You gotta be a nut to play goalie in the National Hockey League," and no one agrees with him more than the men who play goalie in the NHL.

A reporter once asked Johnny Bower, veteran goalie of the Toronto Maple Leafs, what he thought about wearing a face mask. Johnny, who, incidentally, does not wear one, replied this way: "After all, it protects your head and that's where your brains are supposed to be. But sometimes, after standing up against Bobby Hull, I wonder if we have any brains."

It takes a special breed of man to strap himself into 40 pounds of padding, then go out on the ice to act as a clay pigeon for some highly skilled marksman who fires a vulcanized, six-ounce hunk of hard rubber that cuts like shrapnel.

Although their intent was to add more speed and scoring to the game, the NHL board of governors, in the last several years, couldn't have done more to make a goalie's job tougher. In the mid-40s, the NHL introduced the red line. This was supposed to provide more goals for the spectators, but all it succeeded in doing was to change hockey from a pattern passing game into a helter-skelter style of attack which had the poor goalie trying to (1) stop and (2) duck shots he couldn't even see because of the crowd of players that were between him and the shooter. Then, in the '60s, the curved stick was introduced, and if before a goalie couldn't see the puck, now it didn't matter whether he saw it or not, because when it was slapped with a curved stick, there was no way of knowing where it was going to end up. In the hands of a master, such as Bobby Hull, the curved stick can add up to a 125-mile-an-hour shot and can also cause it to do more tricks than a Hoyt Wilhelm knuckle ball.

"Once when I was sitting on the bench," a veteran NHL goalie recalls, "I saw a Hull shot start off knee-high, jump head-high, curve left, land at the goalie's right and skid straight back into the net. And all I did was thank God it wasn't me playing at the time."

Being hit by a flying puck is by no means the only hazard of this job, which has been compared to that of a human target at which rubes fling baseballs in the carnival midway. Because goalies spend a great deal of their time on their hands and knees in front of the nets trying to retrieve loose pucks, they are vulnerable to all sorts of injuries. Hand tendons are cut by skates running over them. Ribs are bruised and cracked by slashing sticks. A head can be laid open if someone accidentally rides a skate into it. Ed Johnston of the Boston Bruins once had his nose broken three times in ten days. Johnny Bower doesn't have a tooth of his own left in his head. Roger Crozier of Detroit has had his jaw broken twice, his left cheekbone broken twice, while it took 25 stitches to repair his neck when someone mistook it for a piece of ice and skated right over it. Terry Sawchuk, veteran goalie for Toronto, has had over 400 stitches taken in his face.

During the last game of the Montreal-Boston semifinal playoff games, Rogatien Vachon, the Canadien goalie, was standing upright, blocking a shot when the very large frame of Ed Westfall, the Bruin forward, came hurtling through the air and crushed Vachon against the goal pipes. From the stands it looked as though the little goalie were dead, and, he admits, that's the way it seemed to him also.

"I thought my back was broken," he recalls. "I lost my breath and it was a long time coming back. I closed my eyes and tried to remain calm, but I was beginning to panic. Then the breath came, but with difficulty. It was a long time before I could breathe right, but I thought it better to stay in the game. I was still warm."

However, with all the mayhem aimed at them on the ice, the goalies agree that they take more from the fans than they do from opposing players.

"The names they call you don't bother me much," said Gump Worsley of the Canadiens, "as long as they keep their hands in their pockets." Unfortunately, many hockey fans don't, and goalies have been pelted by eggs, beer cans, marbles, rotten fish, light bulbs, ink bottles and, believe it or not, a dead turkey (undressed) and a dead rabbit.

If a slap shot off a curved stick hits a goalie in the head, it could be curtains. A few seasons ago, Gump Worsley was hit in the face by one of Bobby Hull's 125-mile-per-hour wallops. He crumbled to the ice, unconscious. When he came to in the dressing room, the first face he saw was Bobby Hull's—Bobby is terrified that one day he will kill a goalie. Worsley suffered only a slight concussion and was back in action when the Canadiens played their next game.

A rifleshot off the stick of Frank Mahovlich once hit Ed Giacomin, goalie for the Rangers, just under the eye. Ed went down like a haymakered heavyweight. For a moment it looked as if he were seriously hurt. But after a few seconds, Giacomin got up; the Ranger trainer put a piece of tape under the eye to stop the bleeding and Giacomin continued to play.

Certainly the physical hurts are the major hazard of the profession, but they are by no means the only hazard. Most hockey men agree that it is the mental strain, resulting from today's power-play hockey and the large number of screened and deflected shots it produces, that has made the job even more difficult.

In 1957, the job of playing goalie reduced Terry Sawchuk to the verge of a nervous breakdown.

In 1951, Bill Durnan, brilliant goalie for the Montreal Canadiens all through the 1940s, hung up his pads, after winning the Vezina Trophy in the 1949–50 season. His nerves were shot from the pressures of the job.

In 1954, Gerry McNeil, also of Montreal, asked for a reprieve in the midst of the Stanley Cup playoffs. He was making $12,000 a year in the NHL but asked to be shipped back to the minors, where he played for half the money. "It wasn't that I was afraid, or didn't want to play," McNeil said. "I was all nerved up and though I tried twice as hard, things just seemed to get worse and worse."

Jacques Plante's wife got an ulcer just *watching* him play.

Glenn Hall of the St. Louis Blues, you'll remember, gets sick to his stomach before every game, even sometimes in the middle of the game.

"Today's goalies have to be so much more agile than they were in the old days," says Jack Adams, former general manager of the Detroit Red Wings, now president of the Central Professional Hockey League. "They have to have much quicker reflexes."

Roger Crozier, Detroit net minder, skated off the ice one night after blowing a game in which they had led 5–1, got dressed and walked out of the locker room, out of the stadium and out of hockey.

"Once you have twelve or thirteen shots against you in a period, you're sucking air," he said. "It's only a matter of time. They had twenty shots and five of them went in. I just said to myself, 'That's it, big boy. Your career is over. That's enough.'"

Later that season, Crozier came back.

According to Jack Adams, Sawchuk is the greatest goalie who ever pulled on the pads. "He was great in the big games," says Adams. In the 1951–52 Stanley Cup playoffs, Sawchuk had four shutouts—three of them in a row.

Hockey men are a strange breed, where the goalie is concerned. Since a goalie's job is to stop goals, not score them, they are almost never given credit when a team wins, but when a game is lost, it's always the goalie who gets blamed.

"If other players make a mistake, it's too bad," says Glenn Hall, "but if we let one in, everyone just assumes it's our fault."

During the 1966–67 season, both Johnny Bower and Terry Sawchuk, the regular goalies for the Maple Leafs, were out with injuries at the same time. Bruce Gamble was called up from the minor leagues to take over the job. And he played well—so well, in fact, that a hockey writer, sensing a story, asked Punch Imlach, then coach of the Maple Leafs, what he thought of the kid. "He's doing what he gets paid to do," said Imlach. "Stop pucks!"

Most hockey men judge goalies not by their good games but by their poor ones. "The goalie who has the least bad games out of seventy, that's the team that wins," says Mel Furer, veteran hockey writer.

If, after all this, you're wondering what would make a man want to play goal, the answer is probably money. A good goalie in the NHL averages around $35,000 a year. Some, like Glenn Hall, make as much as $60,000.

When asked what a man has to have to make the grade

as a goalie, Gump Worsley put it this way: "Goalies should have hard skulls, quick hands and a skin like a rhinoceros. The hard skulls and quick hands will take care of the flying pucks while the thick skin will defy the slings and arrows of critical coaches and customers."

SHORT SHOT

It has been said that a hockey player would beat his own grandmother if she stood in the way of his scoring a goal. No one ever proved it, but then no hockey player has ever had to play against his own grandmother.

But in the 1968–69 season a situation pretty close to the above took place.

Tony Esposito got a goaltending job with the Montreal Canadiens.

His brother, Phil Esposito, was the high scoring center of the Boston Bruins.

And finally it came to pass that brother Phil had to face brother Tony as Montreal and Boston clashed.

Before the game Phil was asked if he'd let up a little considering it was his own brother in the nets.

"You've got to be kidding," Phil said. "Let's get this straight. When it comes to goaltenders—I wouldn't even give my own brother a break."

No one asked him about his grandmother.

18

Upset at Squaw Valley

When an Olympic hockey team doesn't have a regular goalie until a week before its first game, nobody gives it much of a chance.

When an Olympic hockey team, about to enter into competition with some of the best teams from all over the world, is made up of a soldier, a fireman, two insurance salesmen, a TV advertising man and eight players who never played in international competition before, the smart money boys give it even less chance.

And when an Olympic hockey team boils down to little more than a pickup squad—the odds-makers just write it off—no chance.

And that's exactly what everyone gave the U.S. Olympic hockey team in the 1960 Winter Games at Squaw Valley —no chance.

But what didn't show on the form charts were the team's determination, dedication, stick-to-itiveness and will to win.

And win they did, going undefeated against the best teams in the world, and thus creating the biggest upset in the history of the winter Olympic games.

The run for the gold medal started on February 17, in the preliminary trials, when the United States met heavily favored Czechoslovakia. It looked as if the United States would be out of things early; they trailed 4–3 going into the last period. But then the team seemed to come alive. Johnson, on passes from Mayasich and McVey, tied the score 4–4 at 1:58 of the third period. Then Mayasich, a 6-foot, 180-pounder, golfed a shot from the blue line that got past the goalie (his third goal of the evening) for a 5–4 lead. Williams followed with his second goal of the game, and Bill Cleary skated brilliantly through the Czech defense for a solo score.

The following night the United States trounced Australia. This win put them into a six-team championship round robin with Sweden, Germany, Czechoslovakia and highly favored Russia and Canada.

Against the burly but injury-ridden Swedes, the United States jumped off to a 4–0 lead in the first period. Roger Christian fired in the first goal and added one each in the next two periods for the "hat trick." Bob Cleary, McVey and Johnson scored the other goals. Bill Christian received three assists, and Billy Cleary and Williams two each. Jack McCartan, the goalie nobody wanted until a week before the Olympics were to begin, fended off 36 drives, including 15 in the last period.

Upset at Squaw Valley

On February 24, the United States met Germany. It was strictly no contest as the "pickup squad" trounced the Germans, 9–1.

The United States was doing well—but so far the teams they had met were rated no better than they were.

The next big contest was with Canada. And the Canadians, out to avenge their third-place finish in 1956, had assembled the game's fastest group of skaters and roughest back checkers. Man for man the United States didn't stand a chance. According to the experts, they were no match for the determined Canadians. But once again the experts were wrong.

A howling standing room crowd of 8,500 (capacity) in Blyth Arena and millions of TV viewers saw the scrapping, underdog Americans win 2–1 as "last minute goalie" McCartan made one incredible save after another.

"All I could see were streaks of green Canadians," said Jack, who made 39 unbelievable saves.

The United States took a 1–0 lead in the first period when Mayasich fired a slap shot from 20 feet out. It bounced off the stick of Canadian goalie, Don Head, and was slammed home by Bob Cleary at 12:47.

The lead grew to 2–0 when Johnson, a 6-foot, 170-pound Minnesota graduate, intercepted a pass, skated down the left side and scored with a backhand from 35 feet out.

During the furious second period, McCartan stopped some 20 shots, all of them sizzlers. The Canadians poured it on again in the third period but couldn't break through

McCartan's defense until 14:38, when Jim Connelly converted passes from Floyd Martin and Kenny Laufman in a scramble in front of the net.

The United States had come through three games of the round robin tournament undefeated. But could they keep it up? Could McCartan keep up his fabulous defensive work? They were to find out on Saturday, February 27, when they played the highly touted Russian team.

This time 10,000 people fought their way into 8,500-seat Blyth Arena. Millions of TV viewers were tuned in. This was to be the big one.

The United States went out in front at 4:04 of the first period when Bill Cleary took a pass from brother Bob, darted down the right side and slammed the puck past Nikolai Puchlov, the Russian goalie.

But the lead didn't last long.

Less than a minute later Vaniaman Aleksandrov pushed one past McCartan to tie the score. And just four and a half minutes later Mikhail Bychkov fired a bullet that hit the iron bar of the cage, dropped to the ice and bounced into the goal to make the score 2–1 in favor of the Russians.

And the Russians stayed in front until midway in the second period, when Billy Christian, the smallest player on the squad, grabbed a pass from his brother Roger and faked the goalie beautifully for the tying score.

Again, at 14:59 of the last period, Billy Christian foiled the Russian goalie and put the United States ahead 3–2.

And the game ended just that way.

The fans nearly tore down the house. A team that wasn't

even rated a chance was still undefeated after four games, having beaten not only the Canadians but the Russians as well.

In that tremendous effort McCartan used his body, his stick, his hands and his face to keep 27 pucks from getting into the nets.

Only Czechoslovakia—a team the United States had already beaten, but a strong one, nonetheless—stood in the way of an American gold medal. But if the United States lost and the Canadians beat the Russians, it would be Canada, on a goal-spread basis, that would go home with the winner's trophy.

Once again, on February 28, Blyth Arena was packed to the rafters. They came to see the U.S. team take it all. But for the first two periods, the United States just didn't seem to have it. Going into the dressing room at the end of the second period, the pickup squad that had beaten the Canadians and the Russians was trailing 4–3. And even though the score was close, the American team was playing sloppily.

During the intermission, Russia's captain and star defenseman, Nikolai (Solly) Sologubov, who had known many of the American players for some time, came into their dressing room and suggested that they take some whiffs of oxygen to restore their pep. Some of the players took his advice—some didn't.

Whether it was the oxygen or just a flaming desire to win, the American team that came onto the ice in the third period was a determined team, one not to be denied.

At 5:59 of the last period Roger Christian fired the tying marker on a pass from his brother Bill. Then Bob Cleary converted a pass from Mayasich at 7:40 to put the United States ahead. He scored again four minutes later. Roger Christian scored two more goals, and Billy Cleary slipped one more in before the final buzzer.

The United States had beaten Czechoslovakia 9–4.

The pickup team from the United States had won all the marbles.

It was the first time in the history of the Olympic Winter Games that the United States had won a gold medal in hockey competition, proving that sometimes determination and will to win, even more than organization and personnel, are the secret of champions.

SHORT SHOT

In 1927, Pete Muldoon was fired as coach of the Chicago Black Hawks, and when he left, according to sports columnist Jim Coleman, he put the "Curse of the Muldoons" on the Black Hawks.

He told the top brass that the price they would pay for dismissing him would be that they would never win the NHL pennant.

The "Curse of the Muldoons" held up for 40 years.

The Black Hawks finally shook the hoodoo in the 1966–67 season by coming in first over the regular season.

19

Howarth Morenz: The "Girl" Who Became One of Hockey's Great Men

While playing in the junior leagues of Canada, Howie Morenz was so sensational that opposing teams figured it was impossible for anyone so young to be so good. One team even went so far as to look up his birth record. It found that Howarth Morenz was a girl.

"There," they gloated. "If he isn't overage, then why is the team playing him under his sister's birth certificate?"

With this evidence, the Ontario Hockey Association considered the protest but soon dropped the charges when they discovered that a clerical error had been made. The name Howarth was unusual. The clerk who recorded the birth had never heard it before. So instead of asking, he assumed the name to be a girl's and wrote "female" on Howarth's birth certificate.

With the charge about his sex and his age rejected, Howarth, while too smart, too fast and just too good for the leagues, remained a junior.

A great many hockey fans will tell you that Howie Morenz was the greatest hockey player ever. Certainly no one ever had a greater will to win nor did anyone play with greater ferocity.

When Howie finally turned 21, he was approached by virtually every team in professional hockey. He was a player out of the ordinary, another Cyclone Taylor, the star he resembled in so many ways. Naturally the Stratford Club, where Morenz had played as a junior, wanted to retain him for their senior team, but the lure of playing for pay was too much for Howie to remain an amateur.

Leo Dandurand, of the Montreal Canadiens, offered Morenz $850 in cash and a season's contract for $2,500. This was good pay in those days, so Howie signed.

And it didn't take the 5-foot-9-inch, 165-pound center long to convince the pros that he was in the league to stay. Joe Malone, an All-Star in his own right, was the first to recognize that Howie had the mark of greatness. As he later said to a sportswriter: "In the season of 1923–24, I took a look at a new kid in the Canadiens' training camp at Grimsby, Ontario, and I knew right then I was ready for a easy chair. His name was Howie Morenz. In practice he moved past me so fast that I thought I was standing still. I then knew it was time for me to quit."

Morenz won the job as Montreal's center his first year there, and with Aurel Joliat, one of the Canadiens' greatest, at one wing and Billy Boucher at the other, he guided the Canadiens into the Stanley Cup playoffs against the Western champions.

This was a real test for a rookie, but Howie came through like a master. In the first game he picked up a loose puck, swooped down on the Ottawa goal and, with two defenders on his back, slapped the puck right into the twines. The red light lit. It was the only score of the game.

In the second game, in Ottawa, the 21-year-old scored twice. Midway through the first period he picked the puck off an Ottawa player's stick at the blue line, warded off two defenders and then fired a rising shot. The goalie never saw it until it was lying behind him in the net. For an encore, Howie stick-handled the puck from one end of the ice to the other without being touched by an opposing player, then, streaking in front of the goalie, tucked the puck into the corner of the net.

During this playoff series, the Canadiens scored five goals. Morenz accounted for three and assisted on the fourth. In his first year as a pro, Howie Morenz had his name engraved on the Stanley Cup.

There are many stories about Howie's fantastic skating and puck-handling ability. Most of them are true. One of them deals with the time, during a Stanley Cup playoff game, when two defensemen decided they'd had it with Morenz. They were going to get him. On his next rush, if he came up the side, they were going to combine to ram him into the boards. If he came up the middle, they were going to make a Howie Morenz sandwich out of him.

And suddenly, there he was, coming right up the middle. The two defensemen converged on him. Somehow he sensed what they had in mind, for just before he reached them, he poked the puck between them, swerved sharply to the right, circled them, picked up the puck again and blasted a shot past the goalie.

As the puck hit the twines, Howie looked back. There were the two defensemen sprawled on the ice, recovering from the collision.

In 10 years with the Canadiens, Howie Morenz averaged more than 20 goals a season. And this was at the time of 40- and 44-game schedules. Morenz was one of the most brilliant stickhandlers of all time. With the puck stuck to his stick he would rush down the ice. If his path was blocked by defensemen, he would hurl his body into them and somehow come out of the encounter—with the puck still glued to his stick. He would then charge the goalie, feint once and finally put the puck away where it makes the red light light.

The 1929–30 season is generally regarded as the greatest of Morenz's career. He scored 40 goals in a 44-game schedule. (That score would be comparable to scoring 64 goals in a 70-game schedule.) The Canadiens took the Stanley Cup that year and also the next.

Morenz could never bring himself to accept defeat. A loss made him almost physically ill. He became grim and sullen when his team lost. Montreal sportswriter Elmer Ferguson, who knew him well, put it this way: "One night in a playoff game in Boston, the Canadiens lost in overtime when little Cooney Weiland, playing center against Morenz, banged in a long drive. At six o'clock the following morning there came a knock on my door. I opened the portal and there stood Morenz, dressed in his street clothes. It was still dark and a surprised host said a bit testily, 'What's the idea? Where are you going so early?'

" 'To bed,' said Morenz wearily. 'I've been walking the streets all night trying to forget that goal. We lost and it was my fault.'

"And the kid was sobbing."

Try as he could, Ferguson could not convince Morenz that the loss was not his fault. Morenz felt it deeply and took it personally whenever the Montreal Canadiens failed to win.

Morenz was probably one of the biggest contributors to the game of hockey as we know it today. As one writer put it; "Morenz took hockey out of the horse-and-buggy era and propelled it on its way to the days of glory that were to come."

SHORT SHOT

Many a player has turned the hat trick in hockey—scoring three or more goals in one game. But only one player ever turned a lady's hat trick. His name was Butch Bouchard, and it happened this way. The wife of Montreal defenseman Glen Harmon owned one of the more chichi hat shops in Montreal. Mrs. Butch Bouchard, wife of the Canadiens' captain, got a big yen for one of Mrs. Harmon's more expensive creations.

Harmon appointed himself delivery boy—toted the hat over to the Forum and turned it over to Butch Bouchard, telling him that since his wife admired it, he ought to buy it for her.

Butch took one look at the price tag, put it back in the box and told Glen, "No dice."

Harmon then offered to let him have the chapeau free of charge if he scored two goals that night. (In all of the previous season, Bouchard had scored exactly four goals in 40 games. But, somehow, Bouchard rose to the challenge. At the end of the night, the score of the game was Bouchard 2, Detroit 0. Butch had won himself a hat.

It was the first lady's hat trick in the history of hockey, and it took only two goals—not three—to turn it.

20

The Longest Hockey Game Ever Played

On March 24, 1936, in Montreal, the Montreal Maroons and the Detroit Red Wings locked horns in a Stanley Cup playoff game. It was a bone-bruising, hard-checking contest that saw the puck move up and down the ice like a yo-yo, but never once did it go into a net.

At the end of three regulation periods, the score was 0–0.

Another period was played, and still no one was able to score a goal.

The fifth, the sixth, and the seventh periods were equally scoreless.

Near the end of the eighth period, Marty Barry, the Red Wing center, passed to left-winger Herb Lewis. Lewis cut in sharply and fired a shot that should have been the winning goal. It had Lorne Chabot, the Montreal goalie, faked out of his pads. He never even got near it. But it didn't go into the net. It hit the post and was picked up by Maroons' defenseman Hooley Smith.

Hooley started toward the Detroit goal. Part way there, he passed to right-winger Baldy Northcott. Northcott slapped a shot at the Detroit goal. It looked good, but goalie Normie Smith just got a glove on it. Detroit defenseman Doug Young picked it up, cut right, started up ice along the boards, fired a shot which bounced off Lionel Conacher's skate and rolled toward the Montreal goal. Young dove for the puck, but before he could get to it, Lorne Chabot smothered it as the eighth period ended.

That was as close as either team had come to scoring all evening.

After a ten-minute intermission, the ninth period began. And at the 4-minute, 46-second mark, the previous long-game record was broken.

Less than two minutes later, the Maroons launched a four-man power play, but Normie Smith was able to stop them from scoring. Hec Kilrea, Detroit defenseman, picked up the loose puck and, with rookie forward Mud Bruneteau on his right, started up the ice. As they crossed into Montreal territory, Kilrea slipped a pass to Bruneteau, and Bruneteau, who had scored only two goals during the entire season, flashed behind the Montreal defense and, while in full flight, dodged aroud Chabot, who had come out of the net to intercept him, and slapped the puck between the goal posts.

Ninety-five hundred dyed-in-the-wool Montreal fans let out one collective groan.

They had sat in the Forum for six hours, had watched the Detroit goalie, Normie Smith, stop 90 shots without a miss, had watched their own goalie, Lorne Chabot, stop 88 shots without a miss—then lose the game as the 89th shot just did get into the nets. For the Montreal fans it was a most disappointing evening—but they did have the satisfaction of witnessing hockey's longest game.

The final goal was scored at 2:25 in the morning, after 2 hours, 56 minutes and 30 seconds of play.

The record still stands.

SHORT SHOT

It has been said that the job of a Kamikaze pilot is a lot safer than the job of tending goal in the NHL. With curved sticks and slap shots and, worst of all, the screened shot—the bit where one player shoots while another stands in front of him to screen the goalie's vision—the job is becoming more hazardous all the time.

Jacques Beauchamp, a sportswriter for the *Montreal Matin,* a French-language newspaper, used to put on the pads and play goal himself during the Canadiens' practice.

Of all the shooters he faced, he feared Jean Beliveau the most. One day he mentioned this to Terry Sawchuk, who was then the Montreal goalie and one of the tops in the league. "Whenever Beliveau shoots," said Beauchamp, "I just stick out my stick and close my eyes."

"I've got news for you," said Sawchuk. "We all do!"

21

Red Berenson: From Bad to Worse to Great

On November 9, 1968, Red Berenson, star center for the St. Louis Blues, scored six goals in a game against the Philadelphia Flyers—which is six more goals than he scored in the entire 1966–67 season while playing 30 games for the New York Rangers.

He wound up the season with 35 goals, which is only 3 less than he'd scored in 7 previous seasons in the NHL.

For most of his first seven seasons in the NHL, Red Berenson just couldn't do anything right.

In 5 seasons with the Canadiens, he had scored exactly 14 times, and in 2 seasons with the New York Rangers, he had the puck between the pipes exactly twice.

The "Red Baron," as he is called today by the St. Louis fans, was pretty much a bust. In Montreal and New York there were always better centers around—Jean Beliveau, Henri Richard, Jean Lefevre and Phil Goyette. Skating mostly as a penalty killer, Red was just about finished in the NHL. But Scotty Bowman, coach of the St. Louis

Blues, remembered that Berenson had once scored 23 goals in one season while playing for the Hull-Ottawa team. So when he heard that the Rangers were souring on Red, he swapped Ron Stewart to New York for Berenson, even up.

And with Berenson leading the way, the Blues leaped from last place to third place, and into the playoffs. They went all the way to the finals, where they were beaten four straight by Montreal—but every game went into overtime before Montreal won it.

Berenson was almost an instant success with the Blues. He thrived on regular work and the adoration of the St. Louis fans. He scored 22 goals in 55 games in his first part-season with St. Louis, and in 1968–69, wound up as the Western Division's high scorer with 35. Indeed, if there were such a thing as a Most Valuable Player Award for the West, he might have won that, too.

"All I ever wanted was a chance to either play myself into the league, or out of it," Berenson says now. "I was lucky I got an opportunity. Think of all the guys in the past you've heard said had all the ability in the world but never quite developed. How many of them would have had long careers in the NHL if the league had expanded 15 years ago? It scares me to think of just how lucky I've been to get a chance."

Because of his performance with the Blues, Red is now ranked with such stellar centers as Phil Esposito of the Bruins, Jean Beliveau of Montreal, and Stan Mikita of

Chicago. Pretty good company for a guy who didn't score a goal in the 1966–67 season!

"And if he keeps it up four or five more years," says Doug Harvey, one of the greatest defensemen of all time and a guy who should know hockey talent, "he'll be among the greatest."

"Red is far and above the best forward in the Western Division," says his coach, Scotty Bowman. "He plays defensive hockey, too, and besides, he's a class guy. I think he's getting better all the time."

"There just ain't no getting away from it, Red Berenson has developed into one of the better players in the game. What's gotten into him, I don't know," says one of his teammates, "but whatever it is, it should get into everyone of us. We just love the guy."

And so do his bosses. On November 17, 1969, they had a night for the Big Red. The occasion was in honor of the record-equaling six goals in one game. The Red Baron, who is often referred to as the fastest gun in the West, was given a shotgun, a 1969 station wagon and a canoe.

"In New York or Montreal," said Red, who has played for both teams, "all you'd have gotten would have been a handshake."

Even he was amazed by his feat. "I've had two goals on some nights but never three. Stopping the other guy from scoring is my game. This was just out of character for me.

"Scoring the goals was great," Red noted, "but in the

last few minutes I didn't want anybody to score against Jacques Plante [the goalie]. I would have felt like a heel if he had lost his shutout [8–0] while I was trying to score goals."

And the latter part of that statement shows just what kind of a player Red Berenson is. He's shy and introspective; he cares more about his team and his teammates than he does about being a hero.

Even when he phoned his wife about the six goals, he said, "Don't lose your head over it, honey. I hope I don't lose mine."

Berenson gives most of the credit for his success to Scotty Bowman, the St. Louis coach. "When I came to St. Louis," Red has said, "I felt like a kid's bicycle that has two supporting learner's wheels. Scotty took the supports away and gave me a chance to prove I could make it alone. When I knew he had the confidence in me to do a lot of things, I responded to it. I had the chance to open up instead of being inhibited about making a mistake and being pulled off the ice for the rest of the game. But I don't feel I'm a superstar, and I'm not looking for a lot of attention. In fact, I can do without it. When I look at myself, I say I should be shooting better, stick-handling better, checking better and improving the psychological part of my game."

Though he is now near 30, Red figures he has about five or six years of good hockey ahead of him. And, as he told some friends recently, he's going to use those years to achieve his one big goal.

Red Berenson

"Hockey has been good to me," he said, "and the people of St. Louis have been tremendous. I think what I want most in the world right now is to bring a Stanley Cup to the St. Louis Blues fans."

If he keeps scoring and playing the way he has been, he might do just that.

"Hall and Plante keep 'em out, Berenson pops 'em in," is the cry around St. Louis nowadays, and if Berenson keeps popping 'em in, there's no telling just how far the guy who was going nowhere in the NHL is going to go.

SHORT SHOT

. . . And then there's the story of the $300 goalie who helped win a Stanley Cup.

At the end of the 1937–38 season, the Chicago Black Hawks, who had won only 14 games during the regular season, found themselves pitted against the powerful Toronto Maple Leafs in the finals of the Stanley Cup playoffs. The Leafs were top-heavy favorites. Some bookies were even betting that the Hawks wouldn't show up.

Show up they did—but just before the start of the first game, Mike Karakas, the Chicago goalie, who had hurt his toe in a practice session, now found that the toe was broken. He couldn't get a shoe on, much less a skate. Since the teams still carried only one goalie, Chicago coach Bill Stewart had to find a replacement somewhere—and in a hurry.

After a lengthy search, he finally came up with Alfie Moore, a minor league goaltender. Stewart made no attempt to hide from Moore the fact that he was a last resort.

So—Moore went out and played the best game of his otherwise undistinguished career, giving up just one goal as the Hawks won, 3–1. On his way off the ice, Moore thumbed his nose at the Maple Leaf bench.

Back in the Hawks' dressing room, Stewart asked Moore, "How much do we owe you?"

Moore thought it over for a moment, then went as high as he dared. "A hundred and fifty ought to cover it."

Stewart slipped his hero $300. And Chicago, the team that had won only 14 games all season, went on to win the Stanley Cup playoffs.

22

Clear the Track—Here Comes Eddie Shack

In the summer of 1967, Eddie Shack was just about to start a round of golf when a messenger from his team, the Toronto Maple Leafs, reached him on the fairway.

"The Maple Leaf front office would like you to call, it's very important," the messenger told him.

Eddie thanked the messenger, slammed his first shot straight down the fairway and went on to play 18 holes of golf. When he finished, he went to the clubhouse, called the front office and found out he'd been traded to the Boston Bruins.

"What could I have gained by walking all the way back to the clubhouse before I started playing?" he said. "Wherever I had been sent, I had been sent and there was nothing I could do about it."

And this attitude has been typical of Eddie Shack throughout his hockey career. If he can do something about a situation, he does it. If he can't, he doesn't try.

Eddie broke into the NHL back in 1958 with the New York Rangers. The publicity men there labeled him: "The eighth wonder of the world." There was nothing Eddie could do about this tag. He knew he couldn't live up to it—and he didn't. The big city just didn't appeal to Shack, the butcher boy from Sudbury, Ontario—and he never did make the grade.

Traded to Toronto in 1960 for Pat Hannigan and Johnny Wilson, Eddie spent seven knock-down-drag-out seasons with the Maple Leafs. The fans loved Eddie, but as far as Punch Imlach was concerned, Eddie was an entertainer, not a hockey player.

Eddie scored 26 goals in 1965-66, but he spent more time in Punch Imlach's doghouse than all the other players combined. Eddie was inclined to wander out of position, and the word "backcheck" was not in his dictionary.

During this time, Brian McFarlane, noted hockey writer, composed a song entitled "Clear the Track, Here Comes Eddie Shack." This meant that everyone on the ice was in danger when Eddie started throwing his weight around. It has been said that Eddie steers clear of body contact, but one night the hardest check thrown all evening was by Eddie Shack—and it knocked the recipient cold. The recipient, however, was Brit Selby—and he was playing on the same team as Eddie.

The harassed Imlach just shook his head and said, "Eddie, Eddie, Eddie, what am I going to do with you?"

Brit Selby's comments are not printable.

On the subject of hitting, Eddie has this to say: "I like to hit, but remember, it takes more out of you to hit all night and belt guys all over the place. The money goes to the goal scorers and I have a wife and kids."

After two seasons in Boston, where he scored 34 goals and came up with 30 assists, Eddie was on his way to the Los Angeles Kings. And he may yet be just the thing the Kings need.

During their first two years in the NHL, the Kings lacked a spark plug—a no-holds-barred type of guy who can skate onto the ice and stir things up. In Eddie Shack, they've got just that type of player.

Eddie is a crowd pleaser. And if he can duplicate the spectacular fan appeal he had in Toronto and later in Boston, he could become the Toast of the Coast—West, that is.

Los Angeles may be the key to Shack's finally bursting into stardom. In New York he never had a chance. In Toronto the fans dug him, but Punch Imlach didn't. In Boston there were too many young kids looking for his job.

Harry Sinden, the coach of the Boston Bruins, blames the officials for the fact that Eddie Shack still hasn't come into his own. "The way I look at it," said Sinden, "he is barred from the NHL. Every time he goes out on the ice, he gets called for something. It seems that the officials go looking for him. We just couldn't afford to play him."

But if Harry Sinden was glad to get rid of Shack, Red Kelly, coach of the Los Angeles Kings, was delighted to get him. "Eddie is not only colorful, he's good with the puck," Kelly said. "He's rough and he's unpredictable and he can sure stir things up. I never saw anything like the two-minute show he put on against us in Boston one night. He seemed to have the puck the whole time, racing in on our goal, firing sizzling shots and knocking everybody down. Those Boston fans went crazy."

Eddie Shack, who has been called "The Entertainer" and sometimes "The Clown," had this to say about himself. "I never thought of myself as being a clown. If I seemed to be having fun, it was because I really love playing hockey. So I play like I enjoy it. What's wrong with that?"

SHORT SHOT

It had been a particularly tough game.

The penalty box had not been empty from the first minute of play, and the game was now well into the third period. Three major fights had broken out, one of them a near riot. Four players had been removed from the ice and had had stitches taken in their heads.

There had been no let-up, nor was there any in sight.

Up in the stands, in a box reserved for the team's top brass, one of the officials of the Toronto Maple Leafs turned to his companion and said, "If they don't put an end to this sort of thing, we're going to have to print more tickets."

23

World Expansion: Next Step for the NHL?

During the summer of 1969, Cliff Fletcher, chief scout for the St. Louis Blues, went to Europe to sign two hot prospects—Tommy Salmelainien from Finland and Jaroslav Jirik from Czechoslovakia.

These are not the first men of European origin to play in the NHL (Stan Mikita of the Chicago Black Hawks was born in Sokolce, Czechoslovakia), but they are the first big league players to come directly from a European team to an NHL club.

Jirik helped the Czechoslovakian team to two victories over the championship Russian team in World Cup play. And he is the first member of a Czech team ever to be signed to play for another country.

According to Scotty Bowman, general manager and coach of the St. Louis Blues, Europe is the one area that the NHL has not as yet explored for players. And, he adds, if these two men work out, the Blues may do a lot of our scouting in Europe.

Well, if Scotty is thinking of adding more Europeans to his roster, he'd best hurry up and get them, because, according to all indications, it won't be long before the NHL goes international.

Things are already heading that way.

As Clarence Campbell, president of the league, put it: "I would have to say that a game between the NHL and the Russians is getting closer all the time."

Some say it will come within the next two years. The Russians have reigned as world hockey champions for the past seven years and have won gold medals in the last two Olympics.

And after that game is played, what then?

Will the NHL expand to other countries, other continents? Bill Jennings, New York Rangers' president and chairman of the National Hockey League's Expansion Committee, thinks it will.

"Now we have two six-club divisions," he says. "If things go right within the next five years, we may be able to add a third six-club division. Caribbean cities like San Juan, Mexico City, and Caracas, Venezuela [the first steps out of continental North America] will be considered. In the main it will be the role of television which will spread the gospel of the ice sport southward and eventually across the ocean to Europe."

Within a few years, there could be NHL teams in London, Paris, Moscow, Prague, Oslo and Rome.

Does this sound fantastic to you? Well, it could happen.

World Expansion: Next Step for the NHL?

At present, Europe has more registered hockey players than does North America.

Russian and Czech national squads regularly defeat the somewhat reinforced, but still second-rate teams that Canada and the United States send over. The Russians, at present, are ready to challenge the winner of the Stanley Cup, but NHL president Clarence Campbell wants them to play and defeat a minor pro champion first.

"Let's see what they could do with an American League club, then maybe we'll consider it. There also would be the question of which rules we would play the game under." (By "which rules we would play the game under," Campbell was referring to the non-body-contact type of hockey that is played in Europe as opposed to the slam-bang body-checking kind existing under NHL rules.)

Most hockey men, however, feel that if the United States is going to risk its hockey superiority against the Russians, the team that plays them should be composed of All-Stars and should not be a second-rate team from a second-rate league.

Red Kelly, coach of the Los Angeles Kings, says: "Let's have our top players ready for them."

Punch Imlach, ex-manager-coach of the Toronto Maple Leafs, also thinks the game should be played under the rules existing in the NHL today. "I can't wait to see one of those Russians coming over the blue line with his head down and one of our beefy rear guards about to line him up. It should be quite a sight."

Toward this end—a World Hockey League—the NHL is considering hiring some European referees. Clarence Campbell states that the league would hire, for a start, one or maybe even two for a full seven-month season at a regular NHL salary and pay transportation costs to and from North America.

He has suggested this because, as we've noted, the league president feels that games between NHL clubs and European teams will be played very soon and that the biggest problem will be officiating. He says it is virtually impossible to send North American officials to Europe because they are limited linguistically. Europeans have better command of languages. "The only stipulation for the European referees is that they speak English," said Campbell.

Certainly if this world professional hockey league comes off, it will put hockey on an even keel with soccer as an international sport and will lead to gross receipts undreamed of in the early days of the sport.

Just imagine the excitement of the World Stanley Cup playoff if the Moscow Cosmos are pitted against the Montreal Canadiens! The Soviets play as though the future of the communist world depends on their sticks and skates. And as for the Canadiens—well, their commitment to success in hockey knows no bounds, not even family ties.

Not long ago, a Montreal player flubbed an easy shot. And as he went skating down the ice, he could hear his own son giving him the raspberry. Later, when he got home, he asked his son about this and demanded an explanation.

World Expansion: Next Step for the NHL?

"When you score, you're my father," the lad replied. "But when you miss an open goal, you're a bum!"

Yes, the feeling among hockey men is that a world league is not far off. And if a world league is not far off, then a Moscow-Montreal (even a Moscow-New York) Stanley Cup playoff can't be far behind.

SHORT SHOT

Emile Francis, coach of the New York Rangers, played goalie in the NHL for 14 years. He was with a dozen teams but appeared in only 95 games, giving up 355 goals for a 3.74 average.

But though Emile did not rate with any of the top goalies of his time, he was big league in the courage department.

On one occasion, Francis was in the nets against the Chicago Black Hawks. He had a dislocated shoulder, which was strapped into a leather brace.

In the second period a shot whistled in, chin high on his left side.

"Because of the brace," says Emile, "I could not lift my left hand high enough to glove the puck."

"So how did you stop it," a reporter asked him.

"With the only part of my body that was free and could move," he said. "My head!"

The shot split his nose down the middle and knocked out five teeth.

All of which goes to prove that even goalies use their heads sometimes.

24

It Was the Wildest Season Ever: 1969–70

The Boston Bruins, led by stellar defenseman Bobby Orr, copped the Stanley Cup in the 53rd National Hockey League season (1969–70).

They did it in overtime in the fourth game of the finals against the St. Louis Blues, gaining their first Stanley Cup in 29 years.

It was Boston's 22-year-old Bobby Orr who laid St. Louis to rest, with a tremendous goal only 40 seconds after the overtime period had started. And that goal gave the Bruins a 4–3 victory and a 4–0 sweep of the series.

Up to the end the Blues had played inspired hockey— for the first time in the playoff finals. They actually led 3–2 at one point in the final period. But Boston's captain, Johnny Bucyk, tied the game with 6:32 left. And a half-hour later the same Johnny Bucyk circled the Boston Garden ice with the cup in his arms as 14,835 fans roared their approval.

But the crowd had roared louder just seconds before, when Bobby Orr beat the Blues' Larry Keenan to the puck along the St. Louis boards, passed to Derek Sanderson behind the net, took a return pass in front and beat St. Louis goalie Glenn Hall.

"It was a play Sandy and I have worked five or six times this year," Orr said. "When Derek got the pass back to me Glenn had to leave the post and I just shot it and it went through his legs. I was tripped as I shot and when I saw the puck go in I thought I was going to fly across the rink."

Orr did actually fly about ten feet before he fell spread-eagled on the ice. And as he lay there, his teammates piled on top of him.

"Orr made the play by beating Keenan to the puck along the boards," said Sanderson. "That's the confidence he has—to come in from the blue line and take that chance —that no other defenseman in the league has."

The goal was the climax of the series. It was also the climax to the 1969–70 National Hockey League season.

A season that was, without a doubt, one of the craziest in the history of the National Hockey League.

In the strong Eastern Division five of the six teams had a chance for a playoff spot as they entered the final game of the season.

In the Western Division, St. Louis, as expected, walked off with all the marbles. But Pittsburgh, a team mostly made of NHL castoffs, romped home second.

Minnesota didn't have much all year, but they clinched a playoff berth on the next-to-last game of the season with a fluke goal by defenseman Barry Gibbs. The North Stars then won their finale and finished third in the division and thus opposed St. Louis in the first playoff round.

Philadelphia, who rated a threat to St. Louis most of the season, dropped their last two games and wound up out of the money, with Oakland barely beating them out for a go at the playoffs.

In the East, for the second time in NHL history, the Chicago Black Hawks and the Boston Bruins wound up in a flatfooted tie for first place. To settle the tie Clarence Campbell, the league president, invoked an antiquated rule and awarded first place to Chicago on the strength of games won (45–40).

The Bruins, however, lost fewer games than any other NHL team (17), and there's a good possibility that a new rule will be discussed during the off-season.

For the first time in NHL history a Canadian team failed to reach the Stanley Cup playoffs.

The New York Rangers, who led the league for 16 weeks before doing a folderoo in the stretch, sneaked into fourth place in the East on the basis of most goals scored over an entire season—246 to Montreal's 244.

Knowing that New York had beaten Detroit 9–5 in their final game of the season, Montreal coach Claude Ruel yanked his goalie, Rogatien Vachon, and yielded five empty-net goals to the Black Hawks in a futile effort to score more goals.

The Canadiens entered the final game knowing they

needed a win of at least five goals to pass New York. They didn't get them, losing 10–2. Thus Montreal missed the playoffs for the first time in 22 seasons.

In the East the quarter finals for the Stanley Cup started with Boston playing New York and Detroit playing Chicago.

The Black Hawks looked like a team that might take the whole ball of wax when they romped over Detroit, four games to zip.

Boston had a little trouble with the Rangers. They won the first two games in Boston, but then lost the next two in New York. But the second game in New York, which Boston lost, was to be the team's last loss in the entire Stanley Cup playoff.

In the West it was St. Louis vs. Minnesota and Pittsburgh vs. Oakland.

Pittsburgh got by Oakland in four straight. St. Louis went six games before shelving Minnesota, four games to two.

In the semi-finals Boston showed Chicago absolutely no mercy, whipping them four straight (6–3, 4–1, 5–2, 5–4).

The Bruins so bottled up Chicago's Bobby Hull that the Golden Hawk scored no goals and only managed eight shots at the net in the entire series. In the final game Chicago coach Billy Reay switched Bobby Hull from left wing to center, to get him away from Ed Westfall, who had played Hull like an octopus. But even this didn't work, and Bobby got but one shot at the゛goal in the game.

It Was the Wildest Season Ever: 1969–70

The St. Louis Blues had to go all the way to get by Pittsburgh, finally beating them 4–3 in the seventh game of the semi-finals in the West.

And so it was the Boston Bruins vs. the St. Louis Blues in the windup.

The Blues never had a chance. It was Boston all the way. Actually, the entire Stanley Cup playoff was no more than a Boston Tea Party.

Phil Esposito set a Stanley Cup scoring record with 26 points and broke the record for goals with 13.

The Boston line of Fred Stanfield, Johnny Bucyk and Johnny McKenzie surpassed a record for playoff points set in 1955 by Detroit's famous Gordie Howe–Earl Reibel –Ted Lindsay combination.

Boston goalie Gerry Cheevers also set a record with ten consecutive playoff victories.

Bobby Orr broke the record for defensemen in a Stanley Cup playoff, garnering 21 points.

In addition to breaking the scoring record, Bobby Orr won the Hart Memorial Trophy as the Most Valuable Player in the League, the Art Ross Trophy, which is awarded to the highest scoring player in the NHL, and the James Norris Trophy, for being the best defenseman in the league. It was the first time in the history of the game that the Art Ross Trophy and the James Norris Trophy were awarded to the same man.

The 1969–70 season is history now, but it's a cinch that the Boston fans will remember it for a long time to come. So will the Boston team. So will Bobby Orr.